MEN AGAINST WAR

by Barbara Habenstreit ☆

Doubleday & Company, Inc.
Garden City, New York

ISBN: 0-385-02737-0 Trade
       0-385-02746-x Prebound
Library of Congress Catalog Card Number 72–89313

Contents

Introduction

ONE DAY, the poet Carl Sandburg was telling his granddaughter some bloody tales of Civil War battles. He was apparently enjoying these stories more than she, for when he finished, she just sat there looking very grim. Finally she said, "Grandpa, what if they gave a war and no one came?"

Well, there has never been a war when no one came, but in every war some men have always stood up against their governments and refused to serve. Sometimes it was because they were flatly against *all* wars, either for religious, moral, or philosophical reasons. Other times it was because they were against a *particular* war, which they felt was unjust.

In either case, these war resisters were putting their consciences ahead of their countries' policies—and they usually paid a steep price for their beliefs.

This book is about those men—a relative handful in the annals of American history—who would not come when their country "gave a war." It is also about those other men, also pacifists, who eventually abandoned their peaceful ways once they were convinced they couldn't achieve justice without violence.

1 The First Pacifists

A SAVAGE WAR was raging between the settlers and the Indians along the western frontier. The land-hungry pioneers who had made their way across the Appalachians into the Ohio Valley wilderness in the early 1800s, were fighting for their lives against Indian Chief Tecumseh's warriors.

Every frontier village was strongly fortified and guarded around the clock. Stockades were built where settlers from the surrounding area could take refuge in times of attack. Each community was well-armed with muskets, shells, powder, and knives. All the pioneer settlements were geared for a brutal war.

All except one, that is. Over in Busro, Indiana, at the very edge of the western frontier, there was a small commune that was completely unarmed and defenseless. Its members were part of a sect called the Shakers, whose religion forbade them to take part in wars or any other kind of fighting.

The Shakers were different from their neighbors in other ways, too. They believed in sharing all their property, so that no one in the group had any individual possessions. Their land and livestock belonged to all of them, and any money they earned went into a collective purse. They were like a very close-knit family, with their own beliefs, customs, and styles of dress. They kept apart from the other pioneers and tried to have nothing to do with worldly affairs.

But the world would not leave them alone. The other pioneers were very suspicious of the Shaker commune because it was "different," and they were especially angry that the Shakers wouldn't help wage war against the Indians.

Late one afternoon, a rider approached the Shaker settlement with news that the Indians were massing for a large-scale attack. He warned the Shakers to leave their homes at once, get weapons, and rush to the stockade before the assault began.

The Shakers refused. Their lives were in God's hands, they said, and they would have nothing to do with fighting. They continued about their business as if everything was perfectly normal, and the rider left in disgust.

Within a few hours, the Indians descended on the Shaker settlement. Not a single shot rang out, and the neighboring pioneers assumed that the Shakers had been slaughtered without raising a hand to defend themselves.

The Indians took up lodgings in the Shaker village, using it as a base from which to launch their raids. But they didn't remain there very long, for they were soon chased out by United States troops under the command of General William Henry Harrison.

Upon entering the village, the soldiers were amazed to discover that the Shakers were still there—and very much alive. Not a single one of them had been harmed by the

Indians during the entire occupation. In fact, the Shakers said they had been treated very well.

But they fared much worse when General Harrison's troops were quartered with them. The American soldiers seized their livestock and supplies, and used cruel tactics to force Shaker men into the Army. (This practice was finally halted by order of General Harrison.)

Ironically, the Shakers found that the "uncivilized" Indians had more respect for their beliefs than had their fellow Americans. The Indians hadn't hurt them because, as one warrior said later on, "We—we noble warriors! Think we go fight people that hurt nobody? No. We too noble nation for that."

However, the other settlers suspected that the Shakers must have been helping the Indians all along, or they wouldn't have been treated so well. Most pioneers regarded the Indians as inhuman, without any feelings of decency or kindness. If they spared the Shakers, then the Shakers must be traitors.

The hostility and distrust of the other settlers, plus the abuse by the American troops, finally led the Shakers to abandon their commune at Busro. Instead, they joined other, well-established Shaker communes in Ohio and Kentucky. Their old frontier neighbors in Indiana were not at all sorry to see them go.

The Shakers were one of several religious peace sects in America at that time. The others were the Quakers, Mennonites, Dunkers, Brethren, Amish, Rogerenes, and the Schwenkfelders. Their religious views varied greatly, but they all shared the belief that it was a sin to kill their fellow man, even in self-defense. They assumed that the commandment "Thou shalt not kill" meant exactly what it said.

There were other passages in the Bible also that supported their belief:

Resist not him that is evil; but whosoever smiteth
thee on the right cheek, turn to him the other also.
Love your enemies, and pray for them that persecute
you.
Render to no man evil for evil.
Avenge not yourselves, beloved, but give place unto
the wrath of God: for it is written, Vengeance be-
longeth unto me: I will recompense, saith the Lord.
Be not overcome of evil, but overcome evil with good.

Members of the various peace sects were known as
"nonresisters" because they would not fight back even
when attacked; they would not resist evildoers. It might
be thought that they were welcome in America because of
their peaceful ways, but this was never the case. They
were persecuted right from the start.

The Quakers were probably the first nonresisters to set
foot in America. Two Quaker missionaries—Mary Fisher,
a 22-year-old servant, and Ann Austin, a middle-aged
mother of five—sailed into Boston Harbor on July 11, 1656,
on a small ship called *The Swallow*. They had come all
the way from England to plant the seeds of their religion
in the New World; instead, they fell into the hands of
the Puritans.

The Puritan fathers regarded the two women as witches
and kept them prisoner aboard the ship. Their boxes were
searched for "blasphemous" articles, and their books were
burned in the marketplace. Afterward, they were trans-
ferred to prison, stripped bare and searched for bodily
marks of witchcraft. Their ordeal lasted for five weeks,

until finally they were put aboard *The Swallow* once again and deported to the island of Barbados, where a Quaker colony had been established.

Two days after they left, another ship sailed into Boston Harbor carrying eight Quakers. They were jailed for eleven weeks, and then shipped back to England.

But all of this did no good. The Quakers kept coming, and within a few decades their settlements were flourishing in all the American colonies. Although they had been badly abused and persecuted in the early years, the hostility toward them gradually lessened.

However, one aspect about Quakers that Americans couldn't get used to was their refusal to fight. At a time when all the colonies required their men to undergo some military training and to defend their settlements against Indian attacks, the Quakers simply wouldn't take up arms.

Although in a few rare cases these nonresisters were massacred by the Indians, most of the time the Quakers and the Indians got along very well. In addition to their pacifism, the Quakers were required by their religion to be scrupulously honest in their business dealings. They treated the Indians fairly—always paying them a good price for their land and sticking to their agreements—and the Indians respected them in return.

In those colonies where the Quakers had gained some political power, such as Pennsylvania, Rhode Island, New Jersey, and North Carolina, there were almost no Indian uprisings. But in other colonies, where it was common practice to swindle the Indians by getting them drunk and then pushing through unfair bargains, the Indians' resentment was very strong. There were frequent bloody outbursts in which men, women, and children were slaughtered.

However, even during these uprisings, the Indians usually spared Quaker settlements. The Quakers would continue working peacefully on their farms while fighting went on all around them. They would leave their doors unlocked and their homes unguarded, depending only on God for protection. There were many stories of Quakers who traveled unarmed into Indian territory in the midst of an uprising, and were not harmed by any of the Indians they met.

Sometimes, however, the Quakers gave in to their fears and took up weapons to protect themselves. Thomas Story, a Quaker missionary who was traveling around the countryside during the Indian troubles of 1704, told what happened to two Quakers who were out walking together, one with a gun, the other without:

The Indians shot him who had the gun, but hurt not the other. And when they knew the young man they had killed was a Friend [Quaker] they seemed sorry for it, but blamed him for carrying a gun, for they knew the Quakers would not fight nor do them any harm, and therefore, by carrying a gun, they took him for an enemy.

When Quakers were asked to give money for weapons or to help raise a militia to fight the various frontier wars, they always refused. They argued that if the other colonists would treat the Indians better—and look at them as children of God rather than as subhuman savages—there would be no need for weapons and soldiers; there would be no Indian uprisings.

The Quakers practiced this philosophy of brotherhood in their colony of Pennsylvania—their "Holy Experiment" —which was begun by William Penn in 1682 under a land grant from King Charles II of England.

During the seventy-four years that Quakers were in control, Pennsylvania had almost no trouble with the Indians.

However, governing a royal colony posed many other serious problems for a pacifist religious group. The English Crown expected Pennsylvania to raise a militia for defense against the Indians and other enemies, such as the French. But the Quaker Assembly flatly refused to vote money for defense purposes.

Finally, in 1694, the Crown took the colony out of William Penn's control and put it under Governor Fletcher of New York. Fletcher was ordered to raise defense funds, and he forced the Quaker Assembly to compromise on this issue. In the end, they voted money "to feed the Hungrie and Cloathe the Naked," which actually meant buying uniforms and food for soldiers.

In 1696, England returned the colony to William Penn, and the Quakers were overjoyed. However, they knew they had better tread carefully in matters of defense revenues, and regularly voted money for "the King's use" or for the purchase of "bread, beef and pork," which were actually military supplies.

As the years went by, many other groups came to settle in Pennsylvania, and their attitudes toward the Indians and toward warfare were far different than the Quakers'. Also, many of the descendants of the earlier Quakers no longer took their religion so seriously.

William Penn's own children were merely nominal Quakers, and it was they who first began to cheat the

Indians. They wanted to get all the profits they could out of their father's colony, so they manipulated a deal in 1737 in which the Indians were swindled out of a great deal of valuable land. The Indians resented this bitterly, but they bore their grudge in silence for the time being.

The Indians were also brimming with hostility against the Scotch-Irish settlers who were nestling into Pennsylvania's western frontiers, often as illegal squatters. These pioneers heartily disliked the Indians and treated them badly at every turn, so there was mutual malice between the two groups.

By the time France and England went to war over their rival claims in the New World, it was an easy matter for the French to play upon the Indians' rising anger. With French encouragement, the Indians attacked the Scotch-Irish frontiersmen in Pennsylvania, burning their homes, killing and scalping the men, and carrying the women and children off into slavery.

The settlers begged the Pennsylvania Government for military help, but the Assembly was still dominated by devout Quakers who could not bring themselves to dispatch troops. The Assembly did nothing until, finally, the Scotch-Irish made a dramatic protest. They carted their dead into the streets of Philadelphia and dumped the bodies in front of the State House.

This protest, combined with pressure from England, led the Governor of Pennsylvania to declare war against the Indians in April 1756, and to offer a bounty for Indian scalps.

The Quaker members of the Assembly now faced an acute crisis—they either had to wage war or withdraw from the Government. After searching their souls, six Quaker assemblymen finally resigned their political posts, saying: "The present situation of Public Affairs calls upon us for services in a military way, which from a conviction of Judgment, after mature deliberation, we cannot comply with."

This marked the end of seventy-four years of Quaker rule in Pennsylvania. Those Quakers who remained in the Government put their religious scruples aside, so that Pennsylvania was run like any other colony. The "Holy Experiment" was over.

Quakers & Revolution

Perhaps the most severe test for Quakers, and for the other religious peace sects, was the outbreak of the Revolutionary War. Whatever their feelings toward England, the religious pacifists couldn't take part in fighting. If they did, they would be violating their religion.

The Quakers expelled any members who did not remain strictly neutral throughout the fighting. They also refused to pay war taxes or to use the money that was being printed by the new American Government. If they were drafted into the militia, they refused to serve. Nor would the Quakers pay a draft-exemption fee or hire substitutes to fight for them, although many of the other peace sects accepted this as a way out.

Because of their absolute neutrality, the Quakers were suspected of being British sympathizers. To some extent this was true because their faith always demanded obedience to the civil government. No devout Quaker could regard a revolutionary uprising as legitimate, because it involved bloodshed. On the other hand, the Quakers' peace testimony prevented them from taking sides in any battle, so they couldn't aid either the British or the Revolutionaries.

Those Quakers who felt so strongly about the American

cause that they couldn't remain neutral had to leave the Quaker church. Among them was Thomas Mifflin, who later became a Revolutionary general and a governor of Pennsylvania. Betsy Ross, who designed the American flag, was another ex-Quaker. Altogether, about five hundred Quakers were expelled for aiding the Revolutionary cause in one way or another, even if they didn't actually fight. Six Quakers were disowned for joining the British Army.

The Quakers became very unpopular during the war years, and all the old animosity toward them flared up once again. In Philadelphia, forty of the leading Quakers were arrested and asked to swear an oath of allegiance to their new government. But since their religion forbade oathtaking, they couldn't possibly do this. As a result, about seventeen of them were banished from Pennsylvania.

In New Jersey and elsewhere, the Quakers' property was taken away because of their refusal to pay war taxes. Soldiers were quartered in their homes, barns, and meetinghouses, and their livestock was commandeered for military use. Many Quakers were thrown into jail, or pressed into military service against their will and then punished for refusing to handle weapons.

Even after the war was over, the people were so hostile to the Quakers that they often stoned their homes and meetinghouses and chased them through the streets. A sizable number of Quakers who could not cope with this abuse or adjust to the overthrow of the British migrated to Canada after the war ended.

However, the majority remained in the young American republic and gradually adjusted to the new order. In 1789, the Quakers officially reconciled themselves with the

Government by congratulating George Washington on his election as President. However, they still insisted that they could "take no part in any warlike measures on any occasion or under any power."

2 Pacifism Becomes Respectable

NOT LONG AFTER the American Revolution ended, the Napoleonic wars began. They raged through Europe for almost twenty years, so that a whole generation of children grew up without ever experiencing a world at peace. Even the United States, far across the ocean, couldn't escape the holocaust and was dragged into war with England in 1812.

Finally, by 1815, it was all over. The cannons were silenced and soldiers returned to their homes, while the war-weary nations sat down together in hopes of finding a formula for lasting peace. People everywhere were sick of war.

In this atmosphere the first nonreligious peace societies were born. Spawned by the worldwide—but temporary—revulsion against war, small peace groups sprang up simultaneously throughout Europe and America. Whereas pacifism had once been embraced only by the very pious, offbeat religious sects, it now became a fashionable doctrine among worldly and well-to-do intellectuals.

In America the first such peace society took root in New York City. Its leader and founding father was David

Low Dodge, a wealthy merchant who had become an ardent pacifist as a result of several deep personal experiences.

When Dodge was still a child, during the Revolutionary War, he lived on a farm in Brooklyn, Connecticut. The neighboring farm was owned by a man named John Baker, whom everyone regarded as odd because of his outspoken belief that all fighting was contrary to the Gospel. He was not a Quaker or a member of any other pacifist sect, so his belief in nonresistance seemed particularly strange.

When the Revolution erupted, Baker was drafted into the Colonial Army but refused to serve. Branding him a coward and a traitor, his outraged neighbors tried to take him to the Army by force. When he fled into the woods, they pursued him "as hounds would a fox," Dodge recalled. Finally they caught him, tied him up and dumped him into a wagon so that he could be delivered like a prize steer to the troops stationed at Providence, Rhode Island. However, during the journey he managed to cut himself free and escape into the thickly wooded countryside. He hid there all winter, barely surviving through the months of bitter cold and snow.

The cruelty of this episode remained etched in Dodge's memory. Although as a youth he did not share Baker's pacifist views, he had liked this unorthodox, outspoken man whose only crime had been a refusal to harm anyone.

As the years passed, Dodge rose from a poor, unschooled farm boy to a wealthy merchant. He educated himself, became an elder in the Presbyterian Church and a respected member of New York society. Like his friends and fellow church members, he exercised regularly with the militia and often carried firearms; nothing in his religion prevented him from doing this, and although he was a pious man, he was hardly a pacifist.

But one day, while on a business trip, a near tragedy caused him to renounce violence and adopt the same beliefs as his old neighbor Mr. Baker. There had been a series of highway robberies that had led Dodge to arm himself with pistols whenever he traveled. While staying at an inn overnight, he mistook the innkeeper for a robber and very nearly blasted the innocent man to bits.

Dodge was so shaken by this event that he threw away his pistols and relied instead on the protection of God during his travels. After that, he felt relieved. "I was no more tormented with the fear of robbers," he said.

But it would take one more dramatic episode before he would begin spreading the doctrine of nonresistance with evangelical zeal. In 1808, Dodge was felled by an attack of spotted fever. For days he lay near death, and in his delirium it suddenly came to him that all war and all fighting—even in self-defense—were against God's will. He swore that if he lived he would devote the rest of his life to furthering the cause of peace.

This he did. Shortly after he recovered, Dodge published the first non-Quaker pamphlet in America that denounced war as un-Christian and unholy. In it, he said that "all kinds of war, revenge and fighting were utterly prohibited under the Gospel."

The pamphlet caused a small sensation, mainly because its radical ideas were being put forth by a wealthy, respected gentleman who was a pillar of the Presbyterian Church. At that time, all the major Christian churches casually accepted the idea of war, so it was shocking when Dodge—a man of stature—publicly challenged this lack of concern.

Within two weeks, one thousand copies of his pamphlet had been sold, and more were being printed to meet the unexpected demand. Dodge was on his way to becoming one of the leading advocates of pacifism in the United States. Over the next few years he lectured widely, published a book called *War Inconsistent with the Religion of Jesus Christ,* and made many converts. Men of all faiths were drawn to Dodge's pacifist philosophy, for although it stemmed from a deep belief in God, it was not linked to any particular religion. Also, it condemned war for humanitarian reasons as well as for Godly ones, so that a man could remain a Presbyterian or a Methodist and still embrace the new pacifism. This was what made it unique, setting it apart from Quaker, Shaker, Mennonite, or any other sectarian pacifism.

By 1815, when the war with England was over, Dodge felt it was time to set up a society to promote eternal peace. He hadn't wanted to do this while the war was going on, because he thought people might regard such a group as political and unpatriotic. But afterward, conditions were just right, especially since Americans had just had their fill of war.

In August 1815, the New York Peace Society was born. This was probably the first peace society in the world, and certainly the first in America. But at the same time, unknown to Dodge, other peace societies were about to be formed in Massachusetts and across the ocean in England. Pacifism was coming into vogue.

The New York Peace Society, with Dodge as its president, started out with between thirty and forty members, mostly well-to-do New Yorkers, a few prosperous Quakers, and several clergymen of various religions. It was mainly a discussion group, but the members also circulated peace literature and tried to spread their ideas through small gatherings. Within a few years the membership doubled, but the New York society was never to grow much larger than this.

As Dodge later recalled, "My greatest impediment in advocating the doctrines of peace in the United States" lay in "the example of our fathers in the American Revolution."

Eventually, pacifism became far more popular in New England than in New York. Over the years, the Massachusetts Peace Society emerged as the most influential peace group in America, probably because it was less radical than the New York group and did not condemn fighting in self-defense.

Its leader was a Unitarian minister, the Reverend Noah Worcester. Like Dodge, he was not a pacifist in his youth, and had eagerly fought with Washington's Army during the Revolution. But as he grew older, he came around to the view that war and Christianity did not mix.

He felt so strongly about this that during the War of 1812 he found himself unable to offer up prayers in church for an American victory—much to the annoyance of his congregation. Instead, he preached for peace. When he wrote an article entitled "A Solemn Review of the Custom of War," no publisher would accept it. The war was still going on, and publishers were afraid to print anything that attacked the war as unnecessary, un-Christian, and barbarous. In the end, Worcester had to pay for the printing himself, even though he had very little money.

Once the war was over, he founded the Massachusetts Peace Society, which came into being just a few months after the New York society. This group swelled to about one thousand members, with headquarters in Boston and branches in other parts of Massachusetts.

Worcester and Dodge are both regarded as the founders of the American peace movement, even though they never got along very well and disagreed about the morality of fighting in self-defense. Dodge was a total nonresister, while Worcester was not. It was this type of squabbling that prevented the various peace groups from working together for any length of time. By the 1820s there were about fifty such groups, most of them very small, and they all operated apart from one another. When they tried to come together, they ended up behaving like a pack of quarrelsome cats, arguing constantly about how much and what kinds of defensive fighting were permissible. Opinions ranged from the mildest type of pacifism that forbade only aggressive warfare, to absolute nonresistance in which a person could not lift a finger to defend himself under any circumstances.

Finally, this lack of unity began to take its toll. The peace societies started to lose members, until it seemed that the pacifist movement might fade away altogether. To prevent such dissolution, the societies finally managed to put aside their differences long enough to form a large national organization—the American Peace Society.

This was an umbrella-type organization that embraced all forms of pacifism from the most radical to the most conservative. At its founding on May 8, 1828, the Society welcomed "all who seek the abolition of war, whether they hold to the lawfulness of defensive war, or condemn all war in every shape . . . We endeavor to avoid all 'doubtful disputation,' and to walk peaceably with all who will walk with us, whether they go further, or not so far, as the majority of the society."

No peace platform could have been broader, so that the Society's membership ran the gamut from absolute non-resistants to military officers and state officials. They all shared a hatred of aggressive war, but that was just about the only thing they had in common.

The fact that such a mixed bag held together at all was a tribute to the leadership of William Ladd, founder of the American Peace Society and editor of its journal, *Harbinger of Peace*.

Ladd was as unlikely a candidate for pacifism as could be found in the Society. A huge colossus of a man with a quick temper that he tried valiantly to control, Ladd had been a sea captain in his younger years. He was a fascinating speaker, captivating audiences with his easy wit and lusty, salty language—traits that people hardly expected from a pious pacifist.

But then, Ladd had always tended to do the unexpected. As the son of a wealthy New Hampshire merchant, he had been sent to Harvard to become a scholar and a gentleman. He became neither, showing a hearty dislike for his studies and for the conventional life. He did manage to graduate, but immediately set off for sea on one of his father's ships. Other ships and other voyages followed, including one journey on a sloop manned by black seamen, which he undertook in order to study the blacks.

When the War of 1812 made ocean voyages dangerous, Ladd retired from the sea. He had had enough of his aimless, wandering life by this time, and he was ready for something more stable. Settling on his family's large farm in Maine, he became as attached to the lovely rolling countryside as he had been to the sea.

It was at this time, too, that he began to feel a rekindling of the religious fire in his soul—a fire that he thought had burned out years before. He joined the Congregational Church in 1818, and quickly plunged into a new world of humanitarian and philanthropic causes. Among his many concerns were temperance, American Indians, the welfare of seamen, and the antislavery crusade.

Pacifism didn't particularly interest him until one day a friend gave him a copy of Noah Worcester's *Solemn Review of the Custom of War*, one of the most moving and persuasive antiwar tracts of its time. Its message was like a revelation to him, and at the age of forty-one he decided that the cause of peace would be his life's work.

Putting all of his enormous energy into his new-found calling, he roamed the New England Coast seeking to make converts. He lectured wherever he could find a hall or an audience, even if only a handful of people showed up.

In the summer of 1826, Ladd arrived in the town of Newburyport, Massachusetts, where he was to speak at the Congregational Meetinghouse. His audience was small, as usual, but he was in particularly good form that night. His good humor, wit, and kindliness delighted the group, who had been half expecting a stiff and somber lecture from yet another reformer.

Ladd's message was no different from that of other pacifists—that the evils of the world would be over if men could just stop fighting and open their hearts to peace and Christianity. But it was the way he spoke, his earthiness and vitality, that made people really sit up and listen.

In the audience that night was a young man who had just become the editor of the Newburyport *Free Press* three months earlier. He was deeply moved by Ladd's speech, which made him see for the first time that Christian pacifism might be the very tool needed for creating a perfect society. This idealistic, fiery young man demanded nothing less than a morally perfect world, but he was still groping for ways to achieve it.

The next day, his newspaper rang with praises of William Ladd and the new pacifism, which the young editor embraced with the same blind passion he would later shower on other causes. The editor's name was William Lloyd Garrison, soon to become famous for his rousing antislavery crusades in another newspaper, *The Liberator*. But even though Garrison's fanaticism helped spark the Civil War, he himself always remained a pacifist—and such an extreme pacifist that eventually he caused a deep rift within the peace movement.

In those early days, however, Garrison accepted Ladd's brand of moderate pacifism, and the two men became good friends. Ladd went on to found the American Peace Society in 1828, where he proved highly skillful in weaving together opposing points of view. He felt there was room in the Society for all shades of pacifist opinion, and showed great tolerance toward everyone—far more tolerance than many members showed toward each other. Also, Ladd never expected to convert the world to pacifism overnight, which made him a very realistic and temperate leader. He himself had come around to a nearly total nonresistance position, but he didn't try to impose his own views on the Society as a whole.

While Ladd kept trying to unify his warring pacifists, William Lloyd Garrison was getting more involved in the antislavery movement and less concerned with the peace movement. Early in 1831 he began putting out his abolitionist newspaper *The Liberator*. From its columns he spewed forth his hatred of slavery, condemning all slaveholders as evil, sinful thieves. When friends urged him to soften his tone, he refused, saying, "I have need to be all on fire, for I have mountains of ice about me to melt."

But his fierce, uncompromising stand earned him more enemies than followers in those early years, and in 1835 he got his first taste of mob violence—an experience that renewed his zeal for pacifism.

On October 21 of that year, an antislavery meeting was supposed to take place in the Boston offices of *The Liberator*, but when the main speaker didn't show up, the meeting came to an early end.

Meanwhile, a hostile mob, inflamed by the antiabolition Boston press, gathered outside *The Liberator* offices. As people drifted out of the building, the mob taunted and insulted them, and then tore down the antislavery banner that had been waving in the afternoon breeze.

All at once, word spread that Garrison was the only person left in the building. Immediately the mob blockaded the front entrance. Garrison quietly slipped out the back, taking refuge in the loft of a nearby carpenter shop. But the mob had spotted him and was close on his heels. They scaled the ladder to the loft, grabbed Garrison, and were about to hurl him out the window when one of them shouted, "Don't let us kill him outright!"

Instead, they tied a rope around him and dragged him through the streets of Boston, until finally the police stepped in. In the melee that followed, the mob ripped Garrison's clothes off his back. At last the police succeeded in wresting Garrison from his attackers, and locked him in jail for safekeeping on a trumped-up charge of disturbing the peace. He was released the next day on condition that he leave Boston.

Throughout the whole episode, Garrison had never lifted a hand in his own defense. He had a brief opportunity to arm himself and fend off the mob, but he refused. Instead, he had let men hit him, tie him up and very nearly murder him without once striking back. "I will perish sooner than raise my hand against any man, even in self-defense," he had once said. When the test came, he stuck to his beliefs.

Afterward, Garrison became wholly convinced that nonresistance had saved his life. He had depended on God for protection, and God had spared him. Had he put up a fight, both he and his cause would surely have been lost. Garrison was certain now that Christian pacifism was the way—the only way—to achieve moral perfection, end slavery, and wipe out all the other evils of the world. Men could be changed only by spiritual persuasion, never by force, he felt. Such things as political bargaining, negotiation, and compromise meant nothing to him. He saw the battle in moral terms only, and for him there could be no bargaining with evil.

There were many others who shared Garrison's moralistic view of world events. They were the reformers and idealists of their time, the people who took on all worthy causes as their own, and they plunged wholeheartedly into such crusades as abolitionism, pacifism, temperance, and, in some cases, women's rights. Many of the same people were active in all of these movements at once, for their real aim was the perfection of mankind. Almost every pacifist of this era was to some extent also an abolitionist (although not all abolitionists believed in pacifism).

Among the many letters of support Garrison received after the mob attack was one from Angelina Grimké, one of the famed Grimké sisters of South Carolina. Angelina and her sister Sarah were outspoken abolitionists who were soon drawn into Garrison's orbit. They were almost as notorious as he, for they were bold enough to speak out against slavery in public—before male audiences—at a time when all proper ladies were supposed to stay in their kitchens and let men handle worldly matters. But the sisters refused to take a back seat to men, for they were ardent feminists as well as abolitionists.

Even other abolitionists didn't know what to make of these unladylike sisters. Some of them just didn't like the idea of women butting into their movement; they were ready to free the slaves, but they were not about to do the same for women.

Garrison, however, felt differently. He saw that women were oppressed, and he took up their cause as passionately as any other. To him, the Grimké sisters were valuable allies in reforming the world, and he quickly convinced them that the true way lay in total nonresistance and faith in God—as well as a loud voice.

Garrison's radical pacifism appealed to them, for they had become Quakers many years earlier. Although they had grown up in the heady social whirl that was customary for rich southern belles, they despised this frivolous life. Sarah had always longed for an education, but her family denied her one since she was not a boy. Undaunted, she began studying in secret, delving into literature, languages, and law.

The girls' father, Judge John Grimké, was a typical

landed southerner who sometimes treated his slaves harshly. His daughters couldn't stand to see the slaves punished, although they never thought to question the morality of slavery while they were growing up. Nevertheless, Sarah—with her passion for education—taught several of the slaves to read. This was done in utmost secrecy, for educating slaves was strictly against the law in South Carolina.

When the sisters came north to Philadelphia, they were at last freed from the social shackles that bound southern women. Their eager minds opened up to the intellectual ferment around them, and they experimented with several religions. Finally, they decided to become Quakers, and it was under Quaker influence that they took up the fight to free the slaves.

At this stage of their lives, the sisters were well on their way to spinsterhood. Sarah was in her mid-forties and Angelina in her early thirties. By 1835, the sisters had begun giving antislavery lectures before mixed audiences, sometimes speaking as many as five or six times a week. They shared William Lloyd Garrison's pacifist-abolitionist views, and he wholly supported them. Angelina, in particular, was a superb and moving speaker, and she attracted large audiences.

But their forceful presence in the reform movement angered many men. One well-known clergymen openly chided them for participating in men's affairs, saying that if a clinging vine tries to become as independent as an elm, "it will not only cease to bear fruit, but will fall in shame and dishonor into the dust." Another clergyman said that women had a "heaven-ordained role of obscurity."

The sisters would not remain still in the face of such

attacks, and loudly proclaimed that women were the equals of men. "Whatever it is morally right for a man to do, it is morally right for a woman to do," Sarah argued. "All I ask of our brethren is that they will take their feet off our necks and permit us to stand upright on the ground which God has designed us to occupy."

Some abolitionists felt that the sisters should avoid getting into battles over women's rights, for it would take attention away from the antislavery movement. "First, let's free the slaves," they said. "Then we'll get around to women!"

But the sisters remained adamant. "The *time* to assert a right is *the* time when that right is denied," Angelina declared, and she and Sarah went right on speaking their minds in public.

In this way the causes of women's rights, abolitionism, and pacifism were interwoven, so that it was impossible to neatly separate one from another. They were all part of a widespread reform movement.

In 1837, an event took place that made many abolitionists more certain than ever that they must practice absolute pacifism. The episode involved the Reverend Elijah P. Lovejoy, an abolitionist who was also a staunch Garrisonian nonresistant.

Lovejoy had been plagued with troubles for several years. While he was working as the editor of a religious weekly, the St. Louis *Observer,* his antislavery articles infuriated the town's leading citizens. They pressured him to resign, but he refused. When he denounced a particularly brutal incident in St. Louis—the burning alive of a black man—hostile mobs sacked his office.

Lovejoy moved to Alton, Illinois, and tried to start up another newspaper. But his reputation as an abolitionist troublemaker made him very unwelcome in Alton. His first printing press was dumped into the river by a mob before a single issue had been printed. Some of his sympathizers paid for a new press, enabling Lovejoy to put out the antislavery Alton *Observer*. In 1837, mobs again destroyed his press. When it was replaced, they wrecked the new one, too.

The Ohio Anti-Slavery Society bought him still another press—and this time Lovejoy prepared to defend it with weapons. He and his family had been threatened and harassed almost continually, his wife was on the edge of mental collapse, and he himself could stand no more.

In fear and anger, he abandoned his pacifism. He and about sixty other abolitionists got hold of muskets and pistols and took turns guarding the new press. They were sure the mob would be back.

During these tense days, Lovejoy wrote to a friend:

It is now Tuesday night. I am writing by the bedside of Mrs. L., whose excitement and fears have measurably returned with the darkness. She is constantly starting at every sound, while her mind is full of the horrible scenes through which she has so lately passed . . . A loaded musket is standing by my bedside, while my two brothers, in an adjoining room, have three others, together with pistols, cartridges, etc. And this is the way we live in the city of Alton! I have had inexpressible reluctance to resort to this method of defense. But dear-bought experience has taught me that there is at present no safety for me, and no defense in this place, either in the law or the protecting aegis of public sentiment. I feel that I do not walk the streets in safety, and every night when I lie down, it is with the deep, settled conviction, that there are those near and around me, who seek my life . . .

On November 7, 1837, the mob struck. Lovejoy died defending his press, along with several others who were killed and wounded in the fighting.

Elijah Lovejoy became the first martyr of the anti-slavery crusade. However, many abolitionists were shocked at his use of violence, and felt that he might have lived if only he had relied on God's protection instead of gunshot.

Garrison and his followers were especially horrified. Even though they admired Lovejoy's courage in standing up against a mob, they felt that he had rebuffed God by his use of force. In their eyes, it would have been far better if he had died a nonresistant.

In an article in *The Liberator*, Angelina Grimké wrote, "I think I have never received so great a shock to my feelings as in the intelligence of the death of Elijah P. Lovejoy. It was not because an abolitionist had fallen . . . Oh no! . . . It was because he did not fall the unresisting victim of that fury."

In a personal letter to a friend, Sarah Grimké echoed her sister's feelings. "How appalling the spectacle," she wrote. "A minister of Jesus engaging in the work of killing his brother man, of sending to the bar of judgment beings who were mad with fury."

But not all abolitionists felt this way, by any means. Growing numbers of them had come to accept the idea that some violence might be unavoidable in the struggle to free the slaves, although they didn't imagine yet that it could come to civil war.

Lovejoy's death widened the rift between the pacifists

and the nonpacifists within the antislavery movement. It also helped cause a partial breakup of the American Peace Society.

Since its founding in 1828, the Society had been able to accommodate all types of pacifists within its folds. But lately, the Garrisonian wing of nonresistants had been growing very restless. Even though the Peace Society had finally come out against *all* war—even defensive war— the radicals felt that this was not nearly enough. What kind of peace society is it, Garrison asked, that had among its members commanders-in-chief, generals, colonels, majors, and corporals? Any peace group that admitted nonpacifists was "based on sand," he argued.

Lovejoy's death spurred the radicals to break away from the American Peace Society in the fall of 1838 and set up a new group, the New England Non-Resistance Society. Some pacifists refused to have anything to do with this group simply because it dared to admit women on an equal basis with men. But in other ways, too, the group was too radical to have popular appeal. Led by Garrison and his ally Henry C. Wright, the Non-Resistance Society carried pacifism to its utmost extreme—that is, to the point where pacifism sounded very much like anarchism.

The basic premise was that no man—and no government—could ever take a human life without committing a sin against God. Furthermore, all forms of physical force and coercion were wrong, whether practiced by individuals or by nations. The Society scorned all human governments, stating that they were upheld by physical strength, and that their laws were enforced "virtually at the point of a bayonet." This philosophy would have done away with prisons and other forms of legal punishment.

The Society's Declaration of Sentiments, written by Garrison, began:

> We cannot acknowledge allegiance to any human government; neither can we oppose any such government by a resort to physical force. We recognize but one KING and LAWGIVER, ONE JUDGE and RULER of mankind. We are bound by the laws of a kingdom which is not of this world, the subjects of which are forbidden to fight . . . We register our testimony, not only against all war, but against all preparation for war.

The nonresistants felt that men must not hold public office, vote, take part in politics, or support the Government in any other way; nor could they defend themselves or their possessions by force; nor could they sue anyone for redress of injuries; nor could they put anyone into jail. History shows, they said,

> . . . that the sinful dispositions of men can be subdued only by love; that evil can be exterminated from the earth only by goodness; that it is not safe to rely upon an arm of flesh, upon man whose breath is in his nostrils, to preserve us from harm; that there is great security in being gentle, harmless, long-suffering, and abundant in mercy; that it is only the meek who shall inherit the earth, for the violent who resort to the sword are destined to perish by the sword.

Garrison's Declaration of Sentiments proved to be too much even for many of his radical followers. Only twenty-five out of about fifty nonresistants were willing to sign it. Garrison's old friend and fellow pacifist William Ladd disowned the Non-Resistance Society. Although he always remained on good personal terms with Garrison, he didn't want the public to confuse his own American Peace Society with Garrison's radical no-government group. "Many important doctrines of gospel may by pushed to absurdity," he warned.

The Grimké sisters wholly supported the Non-Resistance Society at first, but later on they cooled toward it, partly because of the influence of another abolitionist, Theodore Weld. Angelina had not become a spinster, after all; instead, on her own independent terms, she had married Weld. He was a much more practical and realistic sort of man than Garrison, and the idea of nonresistance and no government did not appeal to him at all. He persuaded Angelina not to try to revolutionize the whole world in one stroke, but to concentrate instead on the struggle to free the slaves. She, in turn, influenced her sister, so that the Garrisonian nonresistants lost two of their main supporters.

Only a hard core of radical pacifists followed Garrison into these new waters, so that the Non-Resistance Society never became very big or important. However, Garrison's Declaration of Sentiments is regarded as a landmark in the history of pacifism. In later times, pacifists like Leo Tolstoy, the Russian author and philosopher, and Mahatma Gandhi, the Indian nationalist leader, would be influenced by Garrison's Declaration.

3 The Mexican War

IF THE PACIFISTS were not united, it was at least partly because they lacked the one thing that was certain to pull them together—a war. Ever since David Low Dodge launched the first peace society in 1815, America and the world had been at peace.

But the idyll came to an abrupt end in 1846, when America went to war with Mexico. This was just the type of war that *all* pacifists could condemn. It was basically aggressive, unjust, and unecessary. Even General Ulysses S. Grant, when writing his *Memoirs* years later, would denounce this war as one of the most unjust ever waged by a powerful nation against a weak one.

The war was the result of America's burning urge to expand. The nation that had begun as a thirteen-state weakling in 1776, had grown fat and powerful by the 1840s. Americans now yearned to extend their empire still more, from ocean to ocean. They felt this was their "manifest destiny," and that they had a God-given right to the lands in the West.

The only trouble was that Mexico was in the way. Mexico owned most of California, Arizona, and New

Mexico. It had also owned Texas once, but the American pioneers who settled there had rebelled against the Mexican Government in 1836, and established Texas as an independent nation.

In 1845, the United States admitted Texas into the Union. This was a prelude to war, for it now seemed painfully clear to Mexico that the United States had designs on the rest of her territory north of the Rio Grande River.

In May 1846, the United States declared war on Mexico.

Although the majority of Americans fully approved of the war, there was a considerable outcry against it—and not just from the peace groups. Many people saw this war as an attempt to gain new territory and extend the limits of slavery, upsetting the fragile balance of power between the slave states and the free ones.

Henry David Thoreau, the poet and philosopher, refused to pay any taxes that might be used to finance the war and aid slavery. For this he went to jail—an experience that led him to write his famous essay *On the Duty of Civil Disobedience.*

Thoreau was not connected with any of the peace groups. He was a highly individualistic man, a loner who preferred to go his own way. He could not easily accept the everyday customs of his fellow men, and even in his youth he was a nonconformist. Upon graduating from Harvard, he would not even accept the diploma. "Let every sheep keep its own skin," he said.

Born in Concord, Massachusetts, Thoreau came from a lower-middle-class family. His father was a pencil-maker, and his mother ran a boardinghouse. Young Thoreau's first love was the world of nature, and after graduating from Harvard he couldn't bear to shut himself up indoors as a businessman or a professional, even though this was all he was trained for. He tried teaching for a while, but soon stopped. Then he began writing poems and essays, only to be faced with the cruel reality that he couldn't make a living this way. To support himself he took odd jobs, working as a day laborer, a mason, a gardener, a house painter, and a carpenter.

In 1845, Thoreau built a small cabin on Walden Pond, where he lived alone for two years, two months and two days. In this serene shelter he contemplated the mysteries and beauties of nature, and worked on his books, essays, and journals. To those who chided him for his nonconformity he said: "If a man does not keep pace with his companions, perhaps it is because he hears a different drummer. Let him step to the music which he hears, however measured or far away."

Thoreau hated slavery, and in the 1840s he stopped paying taxes to the United States Government because he did not want to support a nation that sanctioned slavery. When the war with Mexico erupted, Thoreau reaffirmed his refusal to pay taxes. He viewed the war as an aggressive attempt to expand slavery, and would have nothing to do with it.

One day in 1847, when Thoreau strolled into the town of Concord to pick up his shoes from the cobbler, he was stopped by the sheriff and jailed for nonpayment of taxes. Even though he hadn't paid anything for four years, it was wartime now, and such disobedience was taken more seriously. Now the Government was determined to bring Thoreau into line.

As he sat in the Concord jail staring at the thick stone walls, Thoreau came to the conclusion that jail was "the only house in a slave state in which a free man can abide with honor . . . Under a government which imprisons any unjustly, the true place for a just man is also prison."

Thoreau had no intention of paying his taxes, and might have stayed in jail indefinitely. However, that night, his Aunt Maria rushed to the jail and paid his taxes for him, without his knowledge. In the morning he was released.

Brief as it was, Thoreau's experience in jail had a profound effect on him, leading him to think deeply about man's relationship to the state. Two years later he published his essay *On the Duty of Civil Disobedience,* in which he declared that men *must* refuse to obey immoral laws that clashed with their conscience. The state, he said,

. . . is not armed with superior wit or honesty, but with superior physical strength. I was not born to be forced. I will breathe after my own fashion . . . If a plant cannot live according to its own nature, it dies; and so a man . . .

Must the citizen ever for a moment, or in the least degree, resign his conscience to the legislator? Why has every man a conscience then? I think that we should be men first, and subjects afterwards. It is not desirable to cultivate a respect for the law so much as for the right . . .

A common and natural result of an undue respect for law is that you may see a file of soldiers, colonel, captain, corporal, privates, powder monkeys and all, marching in admirable order over hill and dale to the wars, against their wills, aye, against their common sense and consciences, which make it very steep marching indeed, and produces a palpitation of the heart. They have no doubt that it is a damnable business in which they are concerned; they are all peaceably inclined. Now what are they? Men at all? or small movable forts and magazines, at the service of some unscrupulous man in power . . .

By simply refusing to fight in unjust wars, or to obey unjust laws, men could achieve a peaceful revolution, Thoreau said. "When the subject has refused allegiance, and the officer has resigned his office, then the revolution is accomplished."

The ideas that Thoreau put forth in his essay have influenced history. Martin Luther King, Jr., and his followers practiced civil disobedience by refusing to obey the segregation laws in the southern states. Young men who went to jail rather than fight in Vietnam were also practicing civil disobedience.

Thoreau's hatred of the Mexican War was shared by the poet James Russell Lowell, who wrote a series of sharply satirical, antiwar poems called *The Bigelow Papers*. Lowell, too, believed that men had to obey their own consciences first. As he wrote:

> Ef you take a sword an' dror it,
> An go stick a feller thru,
> Guv'ment ain't to answer for it,
> God'll send the bill to you.

In denouncing all wars, Lowell said:

> Ez fer war, I call it murder,—
> There you hev it plain an' flat;
> I don't wan't to go no furder
> Than my Testyment fer that . . .

Lowell also felt that racism played a part in the Mexican War—that Americans believed that they were racially superior to the Mexicans, so it didn't matter if they took away their lands. This was the same attitude Americans held toward the Indians. They stole Indian lands and casually broke treaties because they didn't really regard the Indians as human. In satirizing this racist attitude, Lowell wrote:

Afore I come away from hum I hed a strong persuasion
That Mexicans worn't human beans,—an ourang outang
    nation,
A sort o' folks a chap could kill an' never dream on't
    arter,
No more 'n a feller'd dream o' pigs that he hed hed to
    slarter;
I'd an idee that they were built arter the darkie fashion
    all,
An kickin' colored folks about, you know, 's a kind of
    national . . .

More than 120 years later, critics of the Vietnam War would also charge that Americans were racists—that they didn't regard Asians as human, and so they didn't feel any pangs about killing them. In both wars, witnesses reported massacres of whole villages, including women and children.

A major difference, though, was that the mass slayings of Vietnamese civilians were regarded as atrocities by most Americans. Newspapers were filled with macabre details of the massacres, and the American soldiers and officers who were responsible were court-martialed (although most of them were acquitted). In contrast, no punishment at all was meted out to lawless American soldiers during the Mexican War, nor was there any great fuss about the reported slayings.

Among the many stories from disillusioned veterans who had fought with General Zachary Taylor was the following account of the sacking of Monterey:

Men, women and children were slaughtered like hogs at a butchering . . . The feeble, the innocent, the helpless, fell beneath his [General Taylor's] sword, and were torn to fragments by his balls and shells. I could hear the shrieks of the dying—the pitiful cries of children over the mangled remains of parents. I saw them crushed, mangled, dying, dead!

Save me from ever witnessing the bombardment and sacking of a city; at least, if I must see it, let there be none but men within its walls. There is some glory in killing *men,* even if they are innocent. This is the soldier's trade and his only way to glory; but there is no comfort nor glory in crushing and mutilating women and children. This is now the trade of Zachary and of every soldier.

This account appeared in an antiwar pamphlet put out by Henry C. Wright, an absolute pacifist who was a close ally of William Lloyd Garrison. Wright was one of the founders of the New England Non-Resistance Society, and one of the fiercest opponents of the Mexican War.

In his pamphlet *Dick Crowningshield, the Assassin, and Zachary Taylor, the Soldier; the Difference Between Them,* Wright charged that the General was no better than a hired assassin who had been paid to murder innocent people. An assassin who murders only one or two people is elevated to the gallows, Wright said, but an assassin who murders thousands may be elevated to the presidency of the United States. (Taylor was elected President in 1848.)

"Let all soldiers and all advocates of war be told that they are murderers," Wright charged, "and let the truth be brought home to them on all occasions, till they feel its force, and then, and not till then, will men learn and advocate war no more."

There was very little censorship during the Mexican War—far less than what occurred during World War I. Antiwar spokesmen printed scurrilous attacks on the United States Government, but the Government tolerated these dissenters with fairly good grace.

William Lloyd Garrison said publicly that he hoped Mexico would win the war. A number of churches took a strong antiwar position, and the American Peace Society bombarded Congress with petitions to end the conflict.

"War is unmoral and depraved; the Army is an unnatural and corrupt organization," stated the *Religious Recorder* of June 23, 1846.

But far more people supported the war, including most of the major religious groups. The Reverend Evan Stevenson, editor of the *Christian Intelligencer and Southern Methodist,* urged the United States to go ahead with the Mexican War, "though it drain the Treasury of the last dime, and make widows of our wives, and orphans of our children."

Newspapers rang with lively debates, and in some areas there were a few small antiwar demonstrations. The town of Syracuse, New York, was the scene of a particularly bitter clash between prowar and antiwar groups.

Touching off the conflict was the following prowar editorial in the Syracuse *Daily Star* on May 26, 1846:

Whatever may be the justice or injustice of the present unhappy state of affairs between the United States and Mexico, we believe no person with an American heart—one who can say and feel, "My country, right or wrong, my country"—can read the intelligence of the progress of arms without a feeling of self-gratification and pride.

Among the antiwar people who took offense at this editorial was the Unitarian minister Samuel J. May. An amiable and tolerant man, May was among the most active reformers of his time. For years he had been involved in peace movements; he was a staunch abolitionist and close ally of William Lloyd Garrison; he worked for women's rights alongside the Grimké sisters, advocated free education for all, and was a leader of the temperance movement and penal reform.

Far from being a fire-breathing dragon of a radical, May was very saintlike. His friends described him as the very model of what a pacifist should be, for he was kind and gentle in everyday life. Lucretia Mott, the Quaker abolitionist, called him "One of heaven's own." Although May was a very good friend of Garrison, he disliked the editor's bitter, frenzied attacks on all who opposed his views. May often urged Garrison to soften his tone, but without any notable success.

May came from a wealthy, socially elite New England family, but he was somewhat of a "black sheep" because of his radical views. In his younger years he remained in the New England area, where the reform movements had their greatest strength. Later on, he moved to Syracuse, New York, to head the Unitarian Church there. He also became Commissioner for the Poor for Syracuse.

When the Syracuse *Daily Star* came out with its prowar editorial, May wrote a letter of rebuttal to the newspaper. Outraged readers responded by calling him a Tory, to which he replied:

Much rather would I be called a Tory than a soldier —a butcher of men. Much rather would I be called a traitor to my country than a traitor to mankind . . . War is the greatest of human crimes, for it includes all others.

The debate raged throughout June of 1846, and it aroused a great deal of friction in Syracuse. Prowar and antiwar factions each called public meetings and abused each other in the press. Other newspapers joined the fracas. On June 14, the Rochester *Advertiser* published an editorial accusing the Syracuse antiwar group of treason:

The village of Syracuse bids fair to be disgraced by a meeting of fanatics, hypocrites and moral traitors who have called a meeting under the imposing caption of "To the Friends of Peace, of Humanity, of the Gospel."

The controversial peace meeting was set to take place on June 18 in Empire Hall, a beautiful new building that had been finished only a short time before. But when the peace group assembled in the hall, they realized at once that enemies were lurking in their midst. Large numbers of prowar people had infiltrated the meeting and were trying to take it over. They immediately proposed a resolution urging strong prosecution of the war. An angry shouting match ensued, until finally Samuel May stood up and asked all the propeace people to leave the hall and reconvene at the Congregational Church.

As they left, a prowar mob, made up of civilians and soldiers on leave, followed them to the church, harassing and taunting them all the way. Even after they were inside the church, the attacks continued. The mob hurled stones through the windows and tried to set the building on fire.

With bedlam raging outside, and stones landing in their laps, the antiwar group drew up a resolution to restore peace and bring American soldiers home from Mexico.

The final blow was that no newspaper in town would print the antiwar resolution.

All this took place at the very beginning of the conflict with Mexico. As the war lingered on—growing very costly and necessitating high taxes—the people's enthusiasm for it rapidly faded. Just one year after the outbursts in Syracuse, the Onondaga *Standard* would write:

> When will the war come to an end is the question at the tongue's end of everybody, and one which is difficult to solve to the satisfaction of all . . .
>
> Still it was desired that the peace should be honorable, but the monetary costs of prosecution of the war led many to want peace at any price. There is an anxious desire among our people to see the war brought to an honorable termination. We can acquire no additional glory by its further prosecution.

The public debt is fast assuming a formidable amount, and the people are becoming surfeited with the interminable details of the battles fought and the victories won, from the area of hostilities.

But the war went on at its own pace until finally, in 1848, it was over. The peace societies and antiwar groups had not been able to prevent the outbreak of the war; nor had they been able to end it or shorten it by their protests. For all their activity, they were powerless.

4 Slavery Must Go!

AFTER 1850, the peace movement in America fell apart. Slavery became the burning issue of the day, and many pacifists threw all their energies into the abolitionist cause. There was no one left to man the peace societies.

The New England Non-Resistance Society withered away, partly because William Lloyd Garrison and others no longer had time for it. They were obsessed with the dream of freeing the slaves.

The American Peace Society grew so conservative that many pacifists wouldn't have anything to do with it. After the death of its founder, William Ladd, in 1842, the Society came under the control of the Reverend George C. Beckwith. Almost immediately he began toying with the idea of softening the Society's declaration against *all* war, and not taking any stand at all on the question of defensive wars. This had been the Society's original position, prior to 1837, and Beckwith wanted to revert to it.

He was supported by the conservative wing of the Peace Society, which soon came to dominate on all policy matters. They would not come out against capital punishment, nor would they lend any support to the idea of personal nonresistance.

In his book *The Peace Manual,* published in 1847, Beckwith outlined the American Peace Society's new official position:

> The cause of peace aims solely to do away [with] the custom of international war, and I trust there will be found in this book nothing that does not bear on this object, nor anything that interferes with the legitimate authority of government. As a friend of peace, I am of course a supporter of civil government, with all the powers requisite for the condign punishment of wrongdoers, the enforcement of law, and the preservation of social order. I deem government, in spite of its worst abuses, an ordinance of God for the good of mankind; nor can I, as a peace man, hold any doctrines imcompatible with its just and necessary powers over its own subjects. I condemn *only* THE GREAT DUEL OF NATIONS.

This meant that the Peace Society would support such things as the use of armed force by the Government to put down a rebellion or subdue a mob. Such a stand meant that it was no longer a pacifist group in any real sense, because it condoned the use of violence by the Government.

From this point on, the American Peace Society became much more respectable in the eyes of the public. It gained a reputation as a "sensible" peace group that didn't mind a little patriotic violence now and then. It concerned itself mainly with inspiring a general interest in world peace, in working for international arbitration of world conflicts, and in supporting the idea of a congress of nations.

But this was simply not enough for the more ardent pacifists in the American Peace Society. The radicals had broken away earlier to set up the New England Non-Resistance Society. Now even the moderate pacifists felt they needed a group of their own.

In May 1847, the moderates organized an American branch of the League of Universal Brotherhood. This was a group that had first been set up in England just a year earlier. Its leader was an American, Elihu Burritt, who had visited England on a peace mission and had stayed to found the League—the first *international* peace society in the world.

Burritt had been a leading member of the American Peace Society, but when it shifted into conservative gear he couldn't support it any longer. He was a true humanitarian who wanted to overhaul all human relationships at once. Wiping out international war was not enough for him. His vision was far broader—he wanted an organization that would also battle slavery and alcoholism, help end restrictions on international trade, and stand up against "everything injurious to the universal interests of man."

While traveling in England, he met many pacifists who shared his views. Their support inspired him to organize a new society then and there—so that instead of staying in England for just three months as he had planned, he remained for almost ten years.

Burritt's League of Universal Brotherhood lured many moderates away from the American Peace Society. Unlike the older group, the League required all its members to be pacifists. Military officers with only a general interest in peace did not qualify. In order to join the League, men had to sign the following pledge disavowing all war and all inhumane acts against other men:

Believing all war to be inconsistent with the spirit of Christianity, and destructive to the best interests of mankind, I do hereby pledge myself never to enlist or enter into any army or navy, or to yield any voluntary support or sanction to the preparation for or prosecution of any war . . . And I do hereby associate myself with all persons, of whatever country, condition or colour, who have signed, or shall hereafter sign this pledge, in a "League of Universal Brotherhood."

At the start, the League had just eighteen members in England, but within a year the membership swelled to about fifteen thousand. The American branch of the League also grew rapidly at first, particularly in New England and the Midwest.

This meant that there were now three separate peace organizations in the United States—one radical, one conservative, one moderate—and all of them fiercely opposed to one another. The radical Non-Resistance Society sneered at the other two peace groups for refusing to follow God's will "all the way." The conservative American Peace Society thought the radicals were madmen, and regarded the League of Universal Brotherhood as nearly useless. As Beckwith said of the League:

It is a fine conception, but altogether too vague and broad for any specific purpose. It covers everything in general, but fixes necessarily on nothing in particular . . . It is one of those vague, magnificent generalities, which for a time enrapture persons of a sanguine, excitable temperament.

The total number of pacifists in America was never very large to begin with, and once they split into three opposing factions, there was no hope that any peace group could grow strong enough to influence national policy.

As the issue of slavery loomed larger on the nation's conscience, people began to lose interest in pacifism altogether. Beginning with the Fugitive Slave Act of 1850, which required the return of runaway slaves who had gone north, and the Kansas-Nebraska Act of 1854, which opened the door to slavery in these vast territories, the nation's attention was riveted on the issue of slavery.

Each crisis drew reformers further away from the pacifist movement and into abolitionist work. Although they still paid lip service to pacifist ideals, many of them came to feel that it would be impossible to end slavery without at least some bloodshed. The lines were being drawn, and pacifists were forced to choose sides.

For those who had believed in absolute pacifism, it was a cruel and bitter choice—to give up their commitment to nonviolence or to give up their dream of freeing the slaves. It had become painfully clear that they couldn't have peace and liberty together.

Most of them chose liberty. One by one, they abandoned their attachment to nonviolence in favor of freedom for the slaves. Their activism took many forms.

In Syracuse, the Reverend Samuel May—once a leading nonresistant—took part in a forceful attempt to free a slave. The incident occurred in 1851 when a fugitive slave—Jerry McHenry—was arrested in Syracuse. While guards held him captive in the police station, May and another abolitionist, Gerritt Smith, plotted a rescue attempt. They organized a mob and set out to capture the police station and overpower the officers.

But May insisted that no weapons be used in the assault, and implored the mob not to hurt the policemen. "If anyone is to be hurt in this fray," he said, "I hope it may be one of our own party."

To everyone's surprise, the assault was successful. The mob freed McHenry, and later smuggled him across the Canadian border. What's more, no one was hurt in the melee.

In writing to William Lloyd Garrison about the famous "Jerry rescue," May tried to explain why he had abandoned his faith in nonresistance. "And let me confess to you," he said, "that when I saw poor Jerry in the hands of the official kidnapers, I could not preach nonresistance very earnestly to the crowd who were clamoring for his release. And when I found that he had been rescued without serious harm to anyone, I was as uproarious as anyone in my joy."

Even before the "Jerry rescue," May had said publicly that men should refuse to obey the Fugitive Slave Law and do all they could to protect runaway slaves. "If you know of no better way to do this than by force and arms, then you are bound to use force and arms to prevent a fellow being from being enslaved," he declared.

May and seventeen others were prosecuted for their role in the "Jerry rescue," but the case was soon dropped. (The northern states were not very enthusiastic about enforcing the Fugitive Slave Law.) Like so many of his pacifist friends, May had not been able to stick to his nonresistance views when faced with a compelling and immediate need to fight slavery.

Gerritt Smith, his coconspirator in the "Jerry rescue," had also been a pacifist at one time. But now he was helping to buy rifles for the free-soil settlers in Kansas, who were having a shoot-out with the proslavery people there.

"Much as I abhor war," Smith said, "I nevertheless believe that there are instances in which the shedding of blood is unavoidable."

The Grimké sisters, too, cast their lot with the militant abolitionists, reluctantly allowing their old pacifist ideals to fall by the wayside. As Angelina said, "We are compelled to choose between two evils, and all that we can do is to take the *least*, and baptize liberty in blood, if it must be so."

The poet James Russell Lowell, who had lashed out so sharply against war in *The Bigelow Papers*, now came to feel that there was no choice but war, if the Union was to be saved and the slaves set free. Now he wrote:

But oh! fair Freedom, if our choice must be
'Twixt war and craven recreance to thee,
Sooner, dear land, let each manchild of thine
Sleep death's red sleep within the enemy's line . . .
Sooner than brook, what only slaves hold dear,
A suppliant peace that is not Peace, but Fear!

In October 1859, John Brown launched his ill-starred raid on Harper's Ferry, igniting the fuse that would soon touch off civil war.

Brown was a very different sort of abolitionist than those who upheld pacifist ideals. He was a fanatic who felt driven to action—ruthless action, if necessary—in order to carry out the will of his angry, vengeful Old Testament God.

In 1857, Brown had met William Lloyd Garrison at the home of a mutual acquaintance. While the other guests listened, Brown and Garrison argued far into the night over the doctrine of nonresistance. Brown rejected it completely, citing bleak prophecies from the Old Testament, while Garrison countered with passages on peace and love from the New Testament. Neither could convince the other of anything, for they each looked to different Gods.

But later, when Brown was tried and executed for his bloody raid, he became a martyr to the abolitionist cause. Even Garrison, one of the last staunch supporters of nonresistance, couldn't hold on to his absolute position any longer. Although he still felt that people who, like himself, *believed* in nonresistance must not fight, he now began saying that it was all right for nonbelievers to take up arms on behalf of justice and righteousness—that is, on behalf of the slave.

Speaking at a memorial ceremony for John Brown in November 1859, Garrison declared:

> I am a nonresistant—a believer in the inviolability of human life, under all circumstances; I, therefore, in the name of God, disarm John Brown, and every slave at the South. But I do not stop there; if I did, I should be a monster. I also disarm in the name of God every slaveholder and tyrant in the world . . . I not only desire, but have labored unremittingly to effect, the peaceful abolition of slavery . . .
>
> Yet, as a peace man—an "ultra" peace man, I am

prepared to say: "Success to every slave insurrection at the South, and in every slave country." And I do not see how I compromise or stain my peace profession in making that declaration.

Whenever there is a contest between the oppressed and the oppressor—the weapons being equal between the parties—God knows that my heart must be with the oppressed and always against the oppressor. Therefore, whenever commenced, I cannot but wish success to all slave insurrections. I thank God when men who *believe* in the right and duty of wielding carnal weapons are so far advanced that they will take those weapons out of the scale of despotism, and throw them into the scale of freedom . . .

Rather than see men wearing their chains in a cowardly and servile spirit, I would, as an advocate of peace, much rather see them breaking the head of the tyrant with their chains. Give me, as a nonresistant, Bunker Hill, and Lexington, and Concord, rather than the cowardice and servility of a southern slave plantation.

With this fiery pronouncement, the peace movement in America finally died.

In April 1861, the Civil War erupted. The American Peace Society saw it as a rebellion rather than a war, and fully supported the use of troops to put down the southern rebels. Most other pacifists put aside their antiwar principles for the duration of the struggle, taking some comfort from Henry David Thoreau's argument that it was morally right to support a war against slavery because it was a "just" war.

Garrison's Non-Resistance Society and Elihu Burritt's League of Universal Brotherhood had just about withered away by this time. When letters were sent out to everyone who had signed the League's antiwar oath, asking if they felt bound by the oath to oppose the Civil War, only two said "yes."

Some former pacifists did a complete turnabout in their fervid support of the war. Midway through the conflict, Sarah Grimké wrote to Garrison: "This blessed war is working out the salvation of the Anglo-Saxon as well as of the African race. The eyes of the nation are being anointed with the eye-salve of the King of heaven . . . This war, the holiest ever waged, is emphatically God's war."

Years before—when no one even dreamed that the slavery issue might lead to civil war—pacifism and abolitionism had gone hand in hand. But in the end, it was impossible to reconcile one with the other, and reformers were torn between conflicting ideals. Forced to choose between a desire for peace and a desire to rid the nation of a grave social evil, most reformers chose the latter.

Only the religious sects remained true to their pacifist beliefs throughout the Civil War. But even among them, there were a considerable number of defectors. The Quakers, in particular, held such strong antislavery views that it was very hard for them to remain neutral during the conflict.

Between two and three hundred young Quakers actually enlisted in the Union Army. One regiment—the 15th from Pennsylvania—became known as the Quaker regiment because it was led by a Quaker colonel, and many of the officers and soldiers were also Quakers.

The great majority of Quakers, however, refused to

fight even when drafted. Nor did they believe it was right to pay a fee to get out of the Army, or to hire others to fight for them. They simply wouldn't have anything to do with war, no matter how noble the cause.

Since it was well-known that the Quakers were strongly against slavery, their fellow countrymen in the North didn't regard them as traitors, but merely as eccentrics. Even so, there were instances when they were harshly abused for their refusal to fight.

In one case, three Vermont Quakers were forced into the Army, and then punished severely because they refused to carry guns or perform medical work in place of military service. Finally, the soldiers took one of the boys, stretched him out on the ground and tied his hands and feet to stakes. They left him this way, first in the broiling sun and then in the rain, for several days.

But a Quaker group in Washington learned of this torture, and sent a protest to President Abraham Lincoln. He intervened in the case and paroled all three boys back to their homes.

Lincoln was generally sympathetic to the Quakers, and claimed that he himself had Quaker ancestors. On many occasions he stepped in to help Quaker conscientious objectors who were being treated unfairly. Lincoln's Secretary of War, Edwin Stanton, was the son of a Quaker, and he, too, sympathized with them. Because of this leniency, the Lincoln administration was sometimes mocked by its enemies as "The Quaker War Cabinet."

However, the Secretary of State, William Seward, didn't feel so kindly toward the Quakers. Once, when two of them came to Washington to plead for some of their fellow Quakers who had been drafted, Seward's anger flared up.

The Quakers, Ethan Foster and Charles Perry, had

been discussing their problem with Secretary Stanton, while Seward sat by in silence. When the meeting was over and everyone was shaking hands, Seward suddenly burst out, "Why don't the Quakers fight?"

Perry replied, "Because they believe it is wrong and cannot do it with a clear conscience."

Seward then reprimanded the two Quakers severely for their refusal to fight, and Foster replied, "Well, if this world were all, perhaps we might take thy advice."

"The way to get along in the next world is to do your duty in this," Seward retorted.

"That is what we are trying to do," said Foster. "And now I want to ask thee one question, and I want thee to answer it; whose prerogative is it to decide what my duty is, thine or mine?"

Seward didn't answer this question, but grew more angry and excited. "Why, then, don't you pay the commutation?" he asked.

The Quakers said they couldn't see any difference between the responsibility of doing an act themselves, and that of hiring another to do it for them.

On hearing this, Seward sprang to his feet and stalked across the room exclaiming, *"Then I'll pay it for you!"* He thrust his hand into his pocket and yelled, "I'll give you my check!"

Foster later wrote, "Immediately after this exhibition, we took our leave in much sadness, at treatment so opposite to what we had expected from Secretary Seward."

The treatment of Quakers in the South was far more severe than in the North. The Quakers were known to harbor antislavery views, and it was suspected (rightly so) that their sympathies lay with the North. Many migrated west during the hostilities, but for those who remained behind, life was very difficult. Although they could have paid a $500 fee for a draft exemption, most of them refused this alternative.

Instead, a number of them fled into the woods to hide. They were safe enough for a while, but as the war dragged on, the South's need for soldiers became more urgent. Every available man was rounded up, and the missing Quaker youths were tracked down like animals. Their families were tortured into giving away their whereabouts, and they were forced into the Confederate Army. If they still refused to bear arms, they could expect to be strung up by their thumbs or "bucked down," that is, tied head to heels for long periods at a time. A number of them died in Confederate Army camps or prisons.

The Quakers suffered rougher treatment than members of other pacifist sects, who were not so openly opposed to slavery or to the war. The Brethren in Virginia, for example, stuck to their pacifism in a far more subtle way. Describing their behavior, the Confederate General T. J. Jackson wrote:

There lives a people in the Valley of Virginia that are not hard to bring to the Army. While there, they are obedient to their officers. Nor is it difficult to have them take aim, but it is impossible to get them to take *correct* aim. I therefore think it better to leave them at their homes that they may produce supplies for the Army.

In the end, the most explosive opposition to the Civil War did not come from pacifists at all. It came from the working classes—the men who actually had to fight the war. They were not particularly peace-loving, and never had been. But they weren't abolitionists either, and this was one war they didn't care for at all, due to both economic fears and race prejudice.

5 The Draft Riots

THERE WERE SIGNS that something was about to happen. New York City simmered with discontent and hostility that lay just under the surface of the everyday clamor. The steamy, soggy July heat didn't help matters any. Tempers were short. Here and there, small groups of people openly defied the authorities over trivial matters, and sometimes there was violence. Yet everyone ignored the warning signs, so that when the holocaust did erupt, the city was totally unprepared.

The immediate cause of the uprising was the new draft law, but this was not the only reason by any means. City laborers had been nursing grievances against the war and against blacks for a long time. Despite all the idealistic talk that the North had gone to war to free the slaves, there were many northern workers who bitterly resented the blacks and were afraid of what would happen once they were free. They certainly didn't want to risk their lives to help free them.

This hostility against blacks was caused by cutthroat competition over jobs. In New York City, free blacks had once dominated certain low-paying occupations. Until the 1840s, they had served as the city's longshoremen, hod carriers, barbers, domestic servants, waiters, and brickmakers. But when the poverty-stricken Irish immigrants began pouring into American cities by the millions during the late 1840s, they crowded the blacks out of these fields. As the two poorest groups in the country, the blacks and the Irish were fierce rivals for the lowest-paying jobs, and the Irish had managed to gain the upper hand. But when the Irish went on strike for better wages, hungry blacks took their places as strikebreakers. Clashes between these two groups often became violent, particularly on the docks.

By the time the Civil War broke out, the blacks and the Irish were implacable enemies—it was the poor against the poor in a struggle for survival. Other members of the white working class were also hostile to blacks because of job rivalry, but none so strongly as the Irish. Such friction was found in many northern cities besides New York.

For these reasons, the war to free the slaves was not overly popular with the northern white working class. They thought it would just intensify the fight for jobs and bring down wages. Also, many laborers were immigrants who had arrived in America only a few years before the Civil War broke out. Political and economic differences between the North and the South meant nothing to them; nor did they particularly care if the states stayed together as one nation or split apart into two. These newcomers had not absorbed enough of American culture, attitudes, and history to care about such strictly American concerns.

Because of the war's unpopularity, the Federal Government had a hard time finding enough men who would willingly go off to fight. This problem became acute as the war dragged on, although it was not apparent at first. When President Lincoln issued his first call for volunteers in 1861, 700,000 men had rushed to sign up. This was an overwhelming turnout—far more than had been expected—so that by the spring of 1862, Secretary of War Stanton ordered all recruiting offices closed. Getting soldiers hardly seemed to be a problem at all.

However, as it turned out, this first group of volunteers represented almost the entire number of patriots who were ready to die to save the Union. Other young men were not so enthusiastic. When a second call for volunteers was issued on July 2, 1862, hardly anyone responded. Within two weeks, Congress was forced to pass a law drafting men into the Army. President Lincoln signed it on July 17, and it became the first *national* draft act in American history.

A national draft was a shocking measure, since all previous wars had been fought by volunteers, mercenaries, and state militias. However, the militias were not reliable, for sometimes they refused to go beyond their own state borders. State loyalties were very strong, and many Americans did not yet feel a deep attachment to their national government. Many of them believed that they had no constitutional duty to defend it. That's why, in their eyes, the national draft was totally un-American and unconstitutional.

In deference to states' rights, Congress had put control of the draft in the hands of the states. Each of them had to supply a certain number of soldiers to the Union Army through their own militia systems.

But such a setup proved to be very slow and inefficient as well as unpopular. There were brief but violent outbursts against the militia draft in Maryland, Pennsylvania, Illinois, Indiana, Ohio, and Wisconsin—leading President Lincoln to suspend the writ of habeas corpus in cases involving draft resisters.

The quota set by the militia draft had been 335,000 men, but in the end, only 60,000 to 70,000 were drafted this way. By March 1863, the militia draft was abandoned as a failure, and a new draft law was passed in its place —this time under Federal authority.

It was this new draft law that set off all the turmoil.

The draft required all able-bodied men between the ages of twenty and forty-five to sign enrollment lists. The names of those enrolled would then be placed in huge lottery wheels, and the drawing would continue until each district's quota was filled. Anyone whose name was picked but didn't want to go could pay $300 for a draft exemption or hire a substitute.

At that time, $300 was almost a year's salary for many workingmen. They couldn't afford to buy their way out of the Army, but the wealthy could. This meant that the draft law exempted the rich, but forced the poor to risk their lives for a cause many of them despised.

Such injustices were the fuel that set off the wild New York City draft riots of July 1863. Hostility to the draft, dislike of the war, blind and bitter racism, and class friction all played a part in the three-day bloodbath that took more lives than any other domestic uprising in American history.

It began with the first lottery that was set to take place in New York City, on Saturday, July 11. For weeks before that, factory workers, porters, longshoremen, and other laborers had milled around on street corners or in taverns, grumbling about the "rich man's war and the poor man's army." They were bitter and resentful, for they had no hope of raising $300; if their names were called, they would have to leave behind families that depended on them, and they would lose their jobs to other men—possibly to blacks, who were draft exempt. The draft threatened to rob them of whatever meager security they had gained, while the rich didn't have to make any sacrifices at all.

The *Daily News*, one of the most popular newspapers in the city, denounced the draft in fiery editorials. Wealthy and influential southern sympathizers, known as Copperheads, also helped fan the discontent, so that by the onset of summer the city was seething.

Some trouble had already developed in getting men to sign the enrollment lists. People were sullen and defiant toward the enrolling officers, insulting them and sometimes threatening them. In one instance, workers who were constructing a building threatened an enrolling officer who had come to take their names. They didn't hurt him, but they succeeded in driving him off.

When he reported the incident, an assistant provost marshal went to the construction site to insist that the workers sign the rolls. The first man he approached raised an iron bar as if to hit him. When the marshal drew his gun, the worker jumped on him and they wound up in a brawl. The rest of the construction crew watched the fight in stony silence. When the marshal got the upper hand, the crew began to advance on him menacingly.

He held them off with his gun for about three hours while he sent passersby to get help, but no one came. Finally, he was forced to leave. The next day he returned with several policemen to arrest the foreman of the crew.

Then the other workers grudgingly signed the enrollment lists.

There were other incidents like this—portents that serious trouble lay ahead. Yet for some reason the city failed to take any extra precautions when the lottery started. Few extra police were put on duty. The Federal troops that had been stationed in New York were not on hand for the drawing—they had been sent away to Pennsylvania to battle General Robert E. Lee's invading forces. Even the Governor of New York, Horatio Seymour, had gone away for the weekend. He didn't seem to be expecting any trouble over the draft.

On the first day, there was no trouble. At 9 A.M., Provost Marshal Charles Jenkins opened the draft office at Third Avenue and Forty-sixth Street, a working-class neighborhood in which one of the first drawings was to start. The draft office occupied the first floor of a four-story brick-and-frame building. On the upper floors were tenement apartments, and next door was a beer saloon.

On this bleak Saturday morning, the draft office was packed with about two hundred men and boys from the surrounding neighborhood. They had come to see what was going on, and most of them were nervously hoping that they wouldn't hear their own names called.

Shortly after 9 A.M., the Provost Marshal signaled for the drawing to begin. A blindfold was placed over the eyes of one clerk, while another clerk turned a crank that made the big drum spin. When the spinning stopped, the blindfolded clerk plucked a folded piece of paper from among the thousands inside the drum. The Provost Marshal read the name out loud—William Jones, from Forty-sixth Street and Tenth Avenue.

The crowd let out a hoot, followed by a lot of jeering

and jesting about poor Willie Jones, New York's first draftee. On the whole, their reaction was good-humored and peaceful, and remained that way for the rest of the morning as hundreds of other names were called. At noon, the Provost Marshal recessed the drawing for the weekend, and many of the crowd drifted into the beer parlor next door.

The next day—Sunday—the newspapers printed the names of the men who had been picked in the first drawing. Almost all of them, from Willie Jones on, were poor factory hands, mechanics and laborers. There were no rich men on the list; they had paid their $300 or hired substitutes to do their fighting for them.

The poorer people had all day to brood about this, since Sunday was their day off; there was no work to take their minds off the injustices they were suffering. In sweltering slum tenements and overcrowded shanties, workingmen sat around drinking their beer, griping to each other and growing furious at the thought of going off to die in place of the rich—while the blacks stayed home and took their jobs.

By the time the lottery resumed the next morning, an angry, disorganized crowd had begun to form outside the draft office. It was made up mainly of the city's poor and underprivileged groups who were about to strike back at the hated draft law with any weapons they could find. Apparently, some of them had the idea of destroying the draft registers that listed their names.

As they converged on the draft office, they gathered up bricks, pipes, sticks, and rocks for their arsenal. All at once, someone threw a brick through a window, and the assault was on!

The mob broke down the doors of the building, invaded the draft office and demolished all the records and furniture. The Provost Marshal managed to escape out the back just as the mob set fire to the building. As the flames shot into the sky, the crowds outside wildly cheered their approval.

Just at that time, John A. Kennedy, Superintendent of Police, happened to be driving past the draft office on his way to police headquarters. When he spotted the flames, he got out of his carriage and ran to the scene of the blaze. Assuming the crowd was just watching the fire, he tried to get past them to see what was going on.

But someone recognized him, shouting, "That's Kennedy!" Instantly the mob turned on him, attacking him viciously. He managed to break away and run, but the mob caught up with him again. They beat him with sticks and bottles, and stomped him until he was bloodied beyond recognition.

A group of men who didn't even know who he was somehow managed to rescue him from the rampaging mob. They rushed him to the nearest police station, where they learned with shock that he was the Superintendent of Police.

But the mob had nearly killed him, and he was in no shape to direct his forces. His assistants had to hurriedly issue orders to combat the growing riot, so the police themselves were in some confusion at first.

Meanwhile, the huge mob was roaming through the streets. They forced factories and shops to close, and got more workers to join them in their furious rampage. Wherever they went, they left destruction in their wake.

In those days, there was no radio or television to spread the news, so most New Yorkers didn't know what

was happening that first day unless they saw it for themselves or heard of it by word of mouth. However, the
police could send messages to all the precincts by telegraph. Once the mob realized this, they tried to cut down
some telegraph poles.

Purely by coincidence, the superintendent of the Telegraph Bureau came across a mob that was chopping down
one of his poles. He hadn't heard about the riot yet, or
about what had happened to the Superintendent of Police;
all he knew was that vandals were attacking the telegraph system. Outraged, he ran up to them and yelled,
"Stop that." The mob surrounded him and held him
prisoner for over an hour while they finished cutting
down the pole. Then they released him, relatively unharmed.

By this time, the original mob of thousands had
broken up into many marauding groups. They thrashed
the first squadrons of police who tried to stop them, and
went on to burn the mansions of the rich, and loot and
set fire to stores. One mob tried to attack the Mayor's
house, but the police drove them back.

In one of the most senseless and cruel assaults, a
crowd set fire to a black orphan asylum, leaving hundreds
of crying, terrified children homeless on the streets of
New York.

The crowds attacked police headquarters, fought
pitched battles with the police throughout the city, put
up barricades and seized the Union Steam Works, where
there were large supplies of carbines. At the height of
the riot, mobs of about 50,000 strong had gained control of a 120-block area in the center of Manhattan, and
were freely wreaking their vengeance on the city. The

New York police were overwhelmed by the wild, surging crowds that kept on plundering, burning, and murdering during the three-day holocaust.

On the second day, the mobs turned their fury on blacks. Any black man, woman, or child who dared set foot outdoors was in danger of being lynched, or worse. When James Costello, a black shoemaker, left his house on an errand, he was set upon by a mob, which first mutilated him and then hanged him. Afterward they dragged his dead body through the streets, smashed it with stones and set it on fire. Still unsatisfied, the mob broke into his home to get his wife and children, but the family escaped out the back and took refuge in a police station.

A great many other blacks were beaten, lynched, mutilated, and burned during the brutal siege. Their homes were broken into and they were not safe anywhere, for the police were almost powerless to protect them. A mob would be driven away from a black home by the police, only to return for their victim after the police had left.

Early on the fourth day, Union soldiers returning from Gettysburg were rushed into New York City to put down the riot. When it was all over, the death count was estimated from a low of 300 to a high of 1200. But it was impossible to get an accurate count, because there were many secret burials. Also, untold numbers of people had been thrown into the rivers, and their bodies were never recovered.

New York was a smoldering, shattered wreck of a city. The mobs had leveled whole streets, taken hundreds of lives, and inflicted millions of dollars' worth of damage, but they hadn't achieved their main purpose. The draft lottery resumed again in August—and the rich could still buy their way out, while the poor couldn't. The riot had not changed a thing.

There were riots in other northern cities, too. Newark, Jersey City, Troy, Boston, Toledo, and Evansville were among many cities that were hit by antidraft and anti-black uprisings, but the New York riot was the bloodiest. After it was over, many blacks moved away from New York out of fear that the wanton murders might start again. By 1865, New York City's black population had declined considerably.

The widespread rioting also had another effect. Government officials began placing less emphasis on the draft as a means of raising an army. Instead, they increased the *bounties* that were given to men who volunteered for service.

The main hope of the draft in the first place had been to prod men into volunteering. The Government itself didn't really like the idea of forcing men into the Army, and hoped to get far more volunteers than draftees. Volunteers were entitled to bounties while draftees were not, so there were advantages in going into the Army willingly. It was the old "carrot and stick" method—but the rioting showed that it might be wiser to rely more on the "carrot" of the bounty than on the "stick" of the draft.

As the war went on, cities and towns across the North tried to fill their quotas without drafting anyone, by offering very high bonuses to volunteers.

In August 1864, the little town of Anneville in New York State offered bounties of $1000 to each volunteer who signed up for three years. In this way, the town was able to meet its quota of twenty-eight men without holding a draft lottery.

Albany was also offering $1000 bounties by this time, but poorer communities couldn't afford that much. Most towns were offering between $500 and $800, so that it was worthwhile for young men to shop around a little before deciding where to sign up. It was only after the richer towns had filled their quotas that the poorer towns were able to attract volunteers.

The bounty system turned into a full-fledged business. There were bounty brokers who steered volunteers to the higher-paying areas, for a hefty commission; agents who were sent out by different towns to round up volunteers; and other middlemen who specialized in finding draft substitutes for well-to-do men. Many of these brokers were totally unscrupulous. There were thieves, scoundrels, and even murderers among them, and they flourished in the confused corruption of the bounty system.

Many of the volunteers, too, were frauds who would say or do anything for the sake of a bounty. There was a classic case of a young woman who disguised herself as a man and tried to enlist for a $900 bounty. However, her hoax was exposed during the physical examination.

Far more common were the bounty jumpers—men who would sign up, collect their bounty, and then desert. Later they would turn up in another town, using another name, and would enlist again for another bounty. They might keep on in this way indefinitely, collecting dozens of bounties. But if they were caught, they could be shot as deserters or sent to the front in chains.

Of course, it wasn't always easy to desert. Many of the worst blackguards in the country had to wear the army uniform for months at a time while awaiting an opportunity to desert. Sometimes these criminals dominated an entire barracks. One young recruit, a sixteen-year-old boy named Frank Wilkeson, described the situation in Troy Road Barracks in Albany, New York. Wilkeson had run away from home to enlist, but army life turned out to be a nightmare for him.

Shortly after he entered the barracks, he was assaulted, robbed, and nearly killed by a group of fellow soldiers, all of whom were experienced bounty jumpers. As an innocent, patriotic youth, Wilkeson was an outcast in a barracks full of thugs. As he told it:

> . . . the social standing of a hard-faced, crafty pickpocket who had jumped the bounty in say half a dozen cities, was assured. He shamelessly boasted of his rascally agility. Less active bounty jumpers looked up to him as a leader. He commanded their profound respect. When he talked, men gathered around him in crowds and listened attentively to words of wisdom concerning bounty jumping . . . His right to occupy the most desirable bunk, or to stand at the head of the column when we prepared to march to the kitchen for our rations, was undisputed. If there was a man in all that shameless crew who had enlisted for patriotic motives, I did not see him . . .
>
> False history . . . says they were brave northern youth going to the defense of their country. I, who know, say they were as arrant a gang of cowards, thieves, murderers, and blacklegs as were ever gathered inside the walls of Newgate or Sing Sing.

Such were the dangers of offering large bounties to men to induce them to fight. Many of the bounty soldiers couldn't care less about who won the war. They were in it only for the money, much like the mercenary soldiers of years before.

On the other hand, it was equally risky to draft men into battle when they didn't really support the cause they were fighting for; the northern draft riots proved this.

The Civil War was probably one of the least popular wars in American history, yet it had to be fought to keep the country together and end slavery. When it was over, the Government had learned some hard lessons about what *not* to do in raising an army. Most important, it learned that a draft law that takes the poor but exempts the rich can be a very dangerous measure, breeding much bitterness and violence.

Yet a little more than a century later, the Government wound up doing the same thing in another unpopular war, only in a more subtle way. This time it was giving draft deferments to college students—who came mainly from the middle classes—while young men who couldn't afford college had to go off to fight in Vietnam. This, too, bred deep resentment on the part of the poor, until finally the draft laws were changed and a lottery system was set up.

Such experiences have shown that the less popular a war is, the more important for the draft system to be fair and democratic—if there *must* be a draft in the first place, which in itself is questionable.

UNPOPULAR THOUGH IT WAS, the Civil War sounded the death knell of the pacifist movement in America. By the time the war was over, pacifism was an outdated philosophy, observed by few worldly people.

The American Peace Society limped along, focusing on the abolition of international wars, and calling for the establishment of an international court of justice to settle conflicts among nations. No one paid much attention at the time.

The only other organized peace society that existed in the post-Civil War decades was the Universal Peace Union, a small radical peace group that had risen from the ashes of Garrison's Non-Resistance Society. Its founder was Alfred H. Love, a Philadelphia wool merchant. Love came from a well-to-do Quaker family, and although he didn't remain an orthodox Quaker, he always clung to his early pacifism.

He was a somewhat eccentric man with a stubborn self-righteousness that made him difficult to get along with. His view of how the world should be was so narrow and rigid that he was never able to attract many followers.

Love was a protégé of William Lloyd Garrison, whom he had met during the Civil War while both were active in a heretical Quaker group, the Progressive Friends. Love called Garrison "my echo and answer to my spirit longings for peace principles."

When he was drafted during the Civil War, Love took his stand as an absolute conscientious objector. He refused to hire a substitute, pay the commutation fee, or even to ask for an exemption because of his nearsightedness. But as it turned out, his eyesight was so poor that the Army decided it didn't want him anyhow.

Throughout the war, Love turned his back on the military. In his business, he refused to handle any orders for the Army, even though this would have been lucrative enough to pull him out of his wartime financial troubles. Also, he refused to pay his militia tax.

In 1866, Love got together with some other pacifists—mainly remnants of the Garrisonian Non-Resistance Society—to form the Universal Peace Union. Love was elected president of the group, which came out for complete pacifism. Christianity never "sanctions war under any circumstances whatsoever," the group declared in its statement of principles.

What made the Universal Peace Union different from Garrison's old group, and from other, earlier peace societies, was that it took a deeper look at one of the root causes of war—economic policies and economic injustices.

The Union believed that "wars are usually inaugurated by the upper and governing classes for the purpose of personal or national ambition," and that these selfish aims meant far more to them than the lives of the fighting men, who came mainly "from the lower and laboring classes."

This observation was drawn most directly from the Civil War, where the working classes were drafted to do the fighting while the wealthy were able to buy their way out.

Because they saw this link between war and economic injustice, the pacifists tried to work for social reform as well as peace. Love—far ahead of his time—called for profit-sharing among workers in industry, and the arbitration of conflicts between workers and capitalists. He also decried the use of force in putting down strikes.

But this did not mean that the Universal Peace Union was pro-labor unions. On the contrary, it distrusted them because of their tendency to use violence. Nor did it favor socialism, although its outlook on the economic causes of war was similar to the socialist position. Basically, the Union was too middle class to fully support organized labor, but it was the first time that any peace society had tried to wipe out economic injustice as a prelude to doing away with war. The Union worked on behalf of the poor ethnic groups, including blacks, American Indians, and all the ragged immigrants from Europe and Asia.

In its more traditional aspect as a peace society, the Union called upon the United States to set an example for the world by getting rid of all armaments at once. It also campaigned hard against capital punishment, and stressed the need to implant pacifist ideals in children. The Union wanted to do away with all warlike playthings for the young, such as toy soldiers and toy guns; end the spanking and beating of children, both at home and in school; outlaw military drills in school; eliminate the war spirit in textbooks; and it discouraged such games as football, which might promote a liking for violence.

At its peak, the Universal Peace Union had about four hundred active members in several branches, as well as about three or four thousand sympathizers. Almost one third of its members were women, including such well-known feminists as Susan B. Anthony, Lucretia Mott, Belva Lockwood (the first woman to run for President), Lucy Stone, and Ernestine Rose. The rival American Peace Society was much less eager to admit women, and didn't allow them to hold office until 1871.

When the Spanish-American War broke out in 1898, the Universal Peace Union was staunchly against it. The Union had been proposing arbitration to settle America's differences with Spain, and it would not support war even after the sinking of the battleship *Maine* in Havana Harbor. For this, the pacifists were regarded as traitors. Alfred Love was burned in effigy in Philadelphia, and his Peace Union came under furious attack in the jingoist newspapers.

This marked the beginning of the end for the Union, for over the next few years its membership dwindled rapidly. When Alfred Love died in 1913, his Universal Peace Union died with him.

If the Spanish-American War killed one peace group, it helped create another. Americans had been roused to passionate support of the war by the sensational newspapers of the day, particularly William Randolph Hearst's *Journal* and Joseph Pulitzer's *World*. As the two newspapers tried to outdo each other in attracting readers, they spotlighted heroic tales of Cuba's rebellion against

Spain, the cruelty of Spanish repression, and the destruction of American property in Cuba. They made it seem that if the United States went to war with Spain, it would be a boon for mankind. America's only goal would be to set Cuba free—or so the newspapers and the politicians said.

But after the United States won the war in just a few months of fighting, new goals emerged. Cuba was liberated, and soon American businessmen were making large profits from Cuban sugar. Moreover, the United States took as its booty from Spain the Philippine Islands, Guam, and Puerto Rico. This only whetted the nation's appetite for expansion, and in 1898 Hawaii was annexed and the Wake Islands were formally occupied. In 1899, the United States and Germany divided up the Samoan Islands.

The Philippines didn't particularly like the change in ownership, and in 1899 they rebelled against their American "liberators." The uprising began as a full-scale revolt, but when it became clear that they were hopelessly overpowered, the rebels switched to guerrilla tactics. The hostilities continued until 1902, when the last rebel leader was caught.

The smashing of the Philippine rebellion was an ugly affair, with many atrocities committed by American soldiers. Afterward, more than eighty United States officers and men were brought to trial for murdering or torturing unarmed Filipino prisoners.

Such events caused many Americans to regret their original support of the Spanish-American War, for now they could see the results. America—the bastion of democracy—was becoming an imperialist power, bent on ruling foreign people without their consent. What had begun as a supposedly humanitarian crusade to free Cuba had turned into an expansionist venture.

Of course, it was not put in such terms by government leaders. In making the decision to deny independence to the Philippines, President William McKinley had said, "I walked the floor of the White House night after night until midnight, and I am not ashamed to tell you . . . that I went down on my knees and prayed Almighty God for light and guidance more than one night. And one night late it came to me . . . that there was nothing left for us to do but to take them all, and to educate the Filipinos, and uplift them and civilize and Christianize them . . ."—and also build a naval base on their islands.

Disillusioned by the final outcome of the Spanish-American War, some Americans turned to a new type of pacifism that had filtered into this country from across the seas. Its apostle was the Russian nobleman and writer Count Leo Tolstoy, author of the epic novel *War and Peace*.

Tolstoy wanted to do away with modern civilization and all the machinery of government, as well as with war. He felt the whole structure of society was based on violence, making it incompatible with Christianity, and he called for a return to the simple life. The way to do this, he felt, was not through politics, but simply by refusing to engage in violence or hostilities of any sort. "The weapon," he said, "is for each man to follow his own reason and conscience."

Tolstoy argued that every man should say to his government, "'You want to make me a participant in murder. You demand of me money for the preparation of implements of murder, and you want me to become a participant in the organized gathering of murderers. But I confess the same law with you, in which not only murder, but even every hostility, has long ago been forbidden, and so I cannot obey you.' It is this means, which is so simple, that conquers the world."

Tolstoy was an absolute nonresistant who scorned all fighting, even in self-defense. Love alone would conquer force and violence, Tolstoy thought, so it was no use calling for international arbitration or world congresses. The Hague Conferences of 1899 and 1907, which laid down rules of international law and conciliation, were of little value in Tolstoy's mind. Similarly, he didn't think much of the establishment of the Permanent Court of Arbitration in 1907—a goal that had been cherished for so many years by the American Peace Society and the Universal Peace Union.

Tolstoy and his followers were removed from politics of all kinds; they withdrew from the game because they were purists who could not bear to negotiate or compromise what they believed in. They wanted to cast away the social and political order altogether.

Tolstoy's views were strikingly similar to those of William Lloyd Garrison, particularly in regard to the antigovernment philosophy and the doctrine of total nonresistance. In fact, Tolstoy often said he was indebted to Garrison, for his own ideas were strengthened when he read Garrison's Declaration of Sentiments.

The first Tolstoy Club in America took root in Boston in 1889. By the early twentieth century, Tolstoy Clubs and colonies were scattered all over. None were very large, but they had a greater impact on American thinking than their size would indicate. Some very prominent Americans—such as William Jennings Bryan, Clarence Darrow, and Jane Addams—were swayed by Tolstoy's ideas, and they carried his message to others. Although none of these Americans accepted Tolstoy's entire philosophy, they looked to him for guidance in their humanitarian and reform efforts.

Among those who made the pilgrimage to Russia to meet Tolstoy was Jane Addams, one of the first American social workers and founder of the Chicago settlement Hull House. She was also a pacifist, and as the twentieth century wore on, she campaigned vigorously to keep the nation out of World War I.

As with so many reformers of her time, Jane Addams grew up in comfortable surroundings and could have led a life of luxury if she had wanted. Instead, she chose to live and work in a settlement house in Chicago's worst slums, where she helped poverty-stricken immigrants carve out a place for themselves in the New World.

Intrigued by Tolstoy's philosophy, and impressed by the simple style in which he lived, Jane Addams visited the Russian nobleman early in the twentieth century. Although Tolstoy was a man of great wealth who owned vast estates, he and his family often worked in the fields alongside the peasants. He had freed his serfs long before serfdom was abolished under Russian law, and he always dressed in peasant clothing.

In writing about her meeting with the aging pacifist, Miss Addams recalled her embarrassment when they were first introduced. Tolstoy, who was wearing a simple peasant shirt, glanced "distrustfully at the sleeves of my traveling gown which unfortunately at that season were monstrous in size. He took hold of an edge and, pulling out one sleeve to an interminable breadth, said quite simply that 'there was enough stuff on one arm to make a frock for a little girl.'"

Feeling like an overdressed mannequin, Miss Addams mumbled a few apologetic explanations. But Tolstoy soon put her at ease, and they settled down for a long talk that made a profound and lasting impression on the American social worker.

Upon returning to the United States, Miss Addams stopped off to visit a Tolstoy colony in the South. The sixty members who lived there practiced absolute non-resistance and had sworn to "obey the teachings of Jesus in all matters of labor and the use of property." According to Tolstoyan principles, they had established a simple, communal sort of society.

On the day Miss Addams came to visit, all the members were busy building a house for a crippled man, his wife, and nine children, who had just come from Arkansas. Since they were the largest family in the colony, they were getting the largest house.

Although the colony was very poor, they gave food and shelter to anyone who needed it, without asking what their beliefs were. When Miss Addams asked if there wasn't a danger that all the paupers in the neighboring poorhouses might flock to the colony for free food, the pacifists replied that this actually had happened during the winter, until the colony's diet of corn meal and cow peas had proved so unappetizing that the paupers had gone back to the poorhouses.

As Miss Addams noted, "even the poorest of the southern poorhouses occasionally supplied bacon with the pone if only to prevent scurvy from which the colonists themselves had suffered. The difficulty of the poorhouse people had thus settled itself by the sheer poverty of the situation, a poverty so biting that the only ones willing to face it were those sustained by a conviction of its righteousness."

The colony lived off whatever meager crops they could grow. The ex-editors, ex-professors, clergymen, artisans, and laborers who had founded the colony spent their days working in the fields and gardens. However, their inexperience with farming, plus their generous, open-handed policy toward all comers, eventually caused the colony to break apart; their everyday struggle for survival proved too harsh for even the most devout believers.

Another Tolstoy follower who made the pilgrimage to Russia was William Jennings Bryan, Democratic candidate for President in 1896, 1900, and 1908. Known as a spokesman for the common man, Bryan waged a lifelong but futile crusade for the free coinage of silver to help the "toiling masses." During the campaign of 1896, he thundered his famous protest against the big-money interests, telling them, "You shall not crucify mankind upon a cross of gold."

Bryan was a latecomer to pacifism. He had reluctantly supported the Spanish-American War, but was thoroughly disgusted afterward when he saw that the United States was turning into an expansionist power. At that point, Bryan took a strong stand against militarism and imperialism—issues on which he waged his second presidential campaign, in 1900. But the American people, who were eager to claim the spoils of the Spanish-American War, rejected Bryan in favor of William McKinley.

Bryan was probably the highest-ranking American to hold deep pacifist beliefs, but his conversion to pacifism was not complete until after his visit to Tolstoy in the winter of 1902–03. Bryan came to the Russian's home at Yasnaya Polyana filled with doubts about the wisdom of nonresistance.

Recalling the meeting afterward, Tolstoy wrote that Bryan, in a gentle and respectful manner, had tried to show him the error of his ways.

[The American] asked me how I would explain my queer attitude as to nonresistance, and, as usual, brought forth the seemingly uncontradictable argument about the murderer who before my eyes kills or outrages a child. I told him that I uphold nonresistance because, having lived seventy-five years, I have never, except in conversations, met that fantastic murderer who before my eyes wanted to kill or outrage a child. But I have constantly seen not one, but a million murderers outraging children and women and adults, old men and old women, and all working people, in the name of the permitted right of violence over their equals. When I said this, my kind interlocutor, with his peculiar quickness of perception, did not give me a chance to finish, but began to laugh and found my argument satisfactory.

Tolstoy convinced Bryan that love was a far more powerful force than violence, and that it could rule the world. When Bryan returned to America, he hung up a picture of Tolstoy in his home, buried himself in the Russian's writings and philosophy, and kept up a correspondence with him. In public, Bryan became a champion of peace and nonresistance—views that fitted in with his deep-rooted, fundamentalist religious beliefs.

Not all of Tolstoy's followers were religious people. Many were total atheists or agnostics whose belief in pacifism sprang from humanitarian impulses, not religion. They were quite different from the pacifists of the nine-teenth century, who believed that God was directing them toward pacifism. In this respect, Bryan—and Tolstoy himself—were more like nineteenth-century pacifists, for their pacifism stemmed from their belief in God.

Tolstoy had a long-lasting influence on Bryan. Later, in 1910, Bryan told an audience:

I suppose that the most significant example in all this world today of one who lives as he preaches this doc-trine of love is the case of Tolstoy. He is not only a believer in the doctrine of love, but he is a believer in the doctrine of nonresistance, and there he stands, proclaiming to the world that he believes that love is a better protection than force; that he thinks a man will suffer less by refusing to use violence than if he used it. And what is the result: He is the only man in Russia that the Czar with all his army dare not lay his hand on . . . The power that is about him, the power that is over him and the power that is in him is proof against violence.

I believe it would be true of a nation. I believe that this nation could stand before the world today and tell the world that it did not believe in war, that it did not believe that it was the right way to settle disputes, that it had no disputes that it was not willing to submit to the judgment of the world. If this nation did that, it not only would not be attacked by any other nation on earth, but it would become the su-preme power in the world.

Ironically, Bryan's hated adversary in later years—
the lawyer Clarence Darrow—was also a disciple of Tolstoy. But Darrow was not concerned so much about war.
His dream was to eliminate crime and violence from
American life, and he believed, as Tolstoy did, that this
demanded a complete restructuring of society. Crime, he
felt, was a "disease" that stemmed from an unjust social
and economic system. Poverty was the cruelest injustice.
Almost equally bad were the coercive institutions—the
police, the Army and the prisons—which relied on force
to keep men in line, but only inspired more violence in
return. If all these injustices were wiped out, Darrow felt,
there would be no more crime and violence; they would
wither away.

Meanwhile, Darrow called for the "complete destruction of all prisons and the treatment of all men as if each
human being was the child of one loving Father." Prisons
only punished; they didn't rehabilitate, Darrow said. He
urged reforms that would combine a minimum of re-
straint with loving care and kindness. Darrow also wanted
to do away with the Army because he believed its main
purpose was to enforce the power of the ruling class
within the state.

Bryan and Darrow each adopted different aspects of
Tolstoy's pacifist philosophy; Darrow applied it to internal
reforms while Bryan applied it to international affairs.
Also, unlike Bryan, Darrow was not a deep believer in
God; in fact, he wasn't sure whether he believed at all.
His pacifism stemmed from his sense of humanity, while
Bryan's stemmed from his faith in God.

Years later, these two men—both so different in so
many ways, yet sharing a passionate concern for the common people—would make nationwide headlines when

they clashed over religion. Darrow, with his rumpled clothes, grimy fingernails, and dark, disheveled hair, stood up in a Tennessee courtroom to defend the teaching of evolution in the public schools. Facing him with bitter hostility was Bryan, a man who took the Bible at face value and was horrified by the idea of teaching children that man might be descended from apes. During the course of this case—the famous Scopes trial—Darrow made a mockery of Bryan's rigid, fundamentalist view of the Bible. Although Bryan won the case, he lost many of his old admirers, who were appalled by the narrowness of his religious thinking.

Darrow was more of a twentieth-century man than Bryan, as were most of the American pacifists who were attracted to Tolstoy's ideas. Their pacifism was tightly bound up with their quest for social justice, particularly economic reform. They wanted to end poverty and bring about economic equality among men. This was Darrow's dream, as well as Jane Addams', and to a lesser extent, William Jennings Bryan's.

But Bryan always remained part of the political establishment, and even rose to the position of Secretary of State under President Woodrow Wilson. Most other pacifists of his day were radical dissenters who veered to the political left. That's why it was so rare to find a pacifist in high government office.

As war clouds burst over Europe in 1914, American pacifists went into a frenzy of activity. Until now, their pacifism had been largely academic and theoretical, for they had come to it after the Spanish-American War; their beliefs had not yet been tested by any new war.

Almost immediately after the hostilities began, a committee of women against the war was formed to protest the slaughter taking place across the ocean. The group's leader was Fanny Garrison Villard—only daughter of William Lloyd Garrison—and even in her old age, as vehement a pacifist as her father had once been.

On August 29, 1914, the women staged a peace parade along Fifth Avenue in New York City. With white-haired Fanny Villard in the lead, several thousand women dressed somberly in black marched slowly down the Avenue. There was no music and no shouting; the women walked in absolute silence, as if in a funeral procession. The only flag they carried was the peace flag. The crowds along the sidewalk were also hushed, for the possibility of war was weighing heavily on everyone's mind.

Even some of the most conservative women's organizations, such as the Daughters of the American Revolution and the National Council of Women, supported the parade. The DAR actually contributed $25 to its cost. (However, the DAR's flirtation with pacifism was very brief; within a year, the Daughters were saying that pacifism was anti-American and possibly traitorous.)

Fanny Villard's son, Oswald Garrison Villard, organized a number of groups to fight the rise of American militarism. Following in the family tradition, Oswald Villard had been championing the cause of peace in the columns of the New York *Evening Post* and *The Nation* ever since the Spanish-American War.

His ardent pacifism so annoyed President Theodore Roosevelt that the old "Rough Rider" once blurted out, "I *wish* that somebody would take Oswald Villard to pieces and forget how to put him together again." Roosevelt also didn't think much of the New York *Evening Post* or *The Nation,* the country's two main left-liberal publications. "What a real donkey the *Evening Post* is," Roosevelt once said. "And what fearful mental degeneracy results from reading it or *The Nation* as a steady diet."

Oswald Villard owned and edited the *Post* from 1897 to 1918, and owned and edited *The Nation* from 1918 to 1932.

Ironically, Villard and Roosevelt resembled each other, for they each had a strong, square-jawed face, a full mustache, and rimless, round eyeglasses. Once when Villard was riding on horseback through New York City streets, he noticed that policemen were saluting and waving at him.

"That afternoon, when I rode onto a Long Island ferry," he said, "I was followed by a motley crowd of commuters and idlers who surrounded me and then stood and stared. Finally, a fireman climbed out of the engine room, walked up to me and said: 'Excuse me, sor, be you Colonel Roosevelt?' When I said 'no,' the crowd promptly disappeared."

Roosevelt was a fighting man who had nothing but contempt for pacifists. He once said, "The man who believes in peace at any price or in substituting all-inclusive arbitration for an army and a navy should instantly move to China. If he stays here, then more manly people will have to defend him, and he is not worth defending."

On another occasion, Roosevelt declared: "The clergyman who does not put the flag above the church had better close his church, and keep it closed."

Oswald Villard's philosophy, on the other hand, was, "To be opposed to war; to hold no hate for any peoples; to be determined to champion a better world; to believe in the equality of all men and women; and to be opposed to all tyrants and all suppression of liberty and conscience and beliefs . . ."

Villard was a leader in many causes, including women's suffrage and black rights. As one of just eighty-four men who marched in a suffragette parade in 1911, he was ridiculed and jeered by many of his own friends. But he came in for far more abuse as a spokesman for black rights, particularly after he helped start the National Association for the Advancement of Colored People in 1909, and served as a member of its Board of Directors.

Because of Villard's reputation as a leading pacifist, Henry Ford came to him for help in launching a "peace voyage" to Europe in December 1915. The automobile titan had not been active in pacifism or politics before, but he was so afraid of American involvement in the war that he had planned a dramatic venture. He had chartered a steamship, *Oscar II*, to take a distinguished group of Americans to Europe, where they hoped to persuade neutral governments to use mediation to end the war. Ford had written to the neutral nations, and said that they had promised him they would listen seriously to his peace group.

Oswald Villard was very skeptical about the venture, feeling that it was a rather naïve idea. However, he agreed to help Ford with publicity, warning him that the press would probably be hostile. But Ford waved aside such caution.

"Oh, I always get on very well with the boys," he said. "All you need is a slogan."

"Yes, Mr. Ford," said Villard, "what kind of a slogan?"

"Oh, something like—'We'll get the boys in the trenches home by Christmas.' What do you think of that?"

Villard thought it was crazy. He argued: "Mr. Ford, there are said to be at least ten million men in the trenches. You have chartered one of the slowest steamers on the Atlantic, and she is not to sail until December 4. If you succeed in stopping the war the day you arrive, which will probably be December 16, it would be physically impossible to march or transport those men home by Christmas."

"Oh," said Ford, "I hadn't thought of that. Well, we'll make it, 'We'll get the boys out of the trenches by Christmas.'"

This was the phrase that became famous throughout the world, although most newspapers played it for laughs. Villard was "disheartened" by the slogan, "for I knew it laid the enterprise open to ridicule; it was already evident to me that he [Ford] had no clear conception of what it was all about, what the war conditions were, or what he was undertaking. Indeed, it gave me a doubt as to his general intelligence . . ."

The voyage was a complete fiasco, ending in a shipboard revolt against Ford by many of his traveling companions. It seems that they hadn't been told exactly what Ford's peace plan was, and were very upset to learn that he didn't really have any. Neither did he have any guarantee that the neutral nations would cooperate.

In recalling the episode later on, Oswald Villard wrote, "There was, I am convinced, no intent to deceive anyone. But those who counseled Mr. Ford, and Ford himself, misinterpreted the purely polite expressions of good will from neutral governments as something vastly more than they signified."

Most of the antiwar groups were far less flamboyant than Mr. Ford's. Among the earliest was the "Henry Street Group," an informal organization that was made up mainly of social workers, a few newspaper editors, ministers, and college professors. Jane Addams was one of the founders of this roundtable discussion group. So was Lillian Wald, director of the Henry Street Settlement House in New York. They and the others agreed to serve as the nucleus of the antiwar movement, and to branch out in response to any prowar activity.

In the coming months, as militant Americans urged President Woodrow Wilson to arm the country in preparation for war, the peace advocates rushed to oppose them. Lillian Wald, Oswald Garrison Villard, Nicholas Murray Butler (president of Columbia University), and Hamilton Holt (editor of *Independent*) helped organize the American League for the Limitation of Armament. This group not only opposed military preparedness, but called for a world federation of nations, with an international congress and an international court to mediate conflicts.

As Miss Wald said, "America's problem is not preparedness for war, but preparedness for peace." President Wilson would later adopt this basic idea for his League of Nations.

Jane Addams founded the Women's Peace Party, and also headed another group that later evolved into the Women's International League for Peace and Freedom. Among the dozens of smaller antiwar groups that sprang up at this time were the American Fellowship of Reconciliation, the National Peace Federation, the World Peace Foundation, the League to Enforce Peace, the Anti-Enlistment League, and the World Patriots. They bombarded Congress with peace petitions, and made the loudest possible hue and cry against war.

President Wilson was torn by opposing forces, but by

the fall of 1915 it was clear that he was leaning toward military preparedness. On December 7, he presented to Congress his National Defense Bill, which included a provision for drafting men into military service.

At this point, several of the antiwar groups decided to unite into one large organization—the American Union Against Militarism (AUAM)—whose main purpose was to defeat the Defense Bill. Its leaders were familiar antiwar spokesmen, including Lillian Wald, Oswald Villard, Jane Addams, and many other prominent Americans.

In less than a year, the AUAM had become the largest peace group in the country, with 1500 active members and thousands of sympathizers. Its antihero and symbol was "Jingo the Dinosaur—All Armor Plate, No Brains." Members of the AUAM carted their huge papier-mâché dinosaur from city to city, as part of a cross-country debate with President Wilson over the Defense Bill.

Not all the opponents of the Defense Bill were pacifists, however; there was violent opposition as well. In San Francisco, someone set off a bomb at a Military Preparedness Day parade, killing and wounding many people. A man named Tom Mooney spent more than twenty years in jail for this act, even though there was strong evidence that he had been convicted unjustly. The Mooney case became a *cause célèbre* from coast to coast, with many civil rights leaders coming to his defense. Eventually, Mooney was pardoned by the Governor of California.

Regardless of the uproar, Congress passed the Defense Bill. However, it left out the provision that the pacifists had objected to most strongly—the draft.

For a time after that, all was quiet. Then, in February

1917, Germany announced that it would resume unrestricted submarine warfare, with neutrals as well as enemies. This had been a bitter issue between the United States and Germany, and the sudden announcement caused President Wilson to break off diplomatic ties.

Wilson had tried his best to keep America out of the world conflict. He had been re-elected in 1916 on the slogan, "He Kept Us Out of War." But on April 6, 1917, as a result of "the irresistible logic of events," the United States declared war on Germany.

From then on, the pacifists began to scatter in all directions. Norman Thomas, who had just begun his long career as a socialist and pacifist, was amazed at how quickly the many peace groups broke up. "It still remains somewhat surprising," he wrote later, "not that they disappeared, but that they vanished so easily, completely and finally, before the Government had time to take really aggressive action against them."

For most pacifists, the actual outbreak of war meant that they had to abandon their pacifism and support their country; to do otherwise was unthinkable.

Clarence Darrow, an early pacifist, had a complete change of heart as far as international war was concerned. Writing his biography years later, he recalled:

For many years I had been an ardent reader of Tolstoy, and regarded myself as one of his disciples. When Germany invaded Belgium, I recovered from my pacifism in the twinkling of an eye. It came to me through my emotions, and it left me the same way. I discovered that pacifism is probably a good doctrine in time of peace, but of no value in time of war.

Darrow had come so far from pacifism that he could even write:

> The pacifist speaks with the German accent. Even if his words are not against America, the import of all he says is to aid Germany against America and its allies in the war.

However, as one of America's leading civil-liberties lawyers, Darrow did defend conscientious objectors during the war. He didn't want to see them deprived of their rights, even though he no longer shared their beliefs.

William Jennings Bryan was another pacifist who supported the war, but in his case it was not surprising. Bryan was a true believer in the doctrine of majority rule, and he thought it was wrong for any individual in a democracy to pit himself against the popular will *once a decision had been made*.

Bryan had tried his best to convert the majority of Americans to his own pacifist outlook. He had even resigned as Secretary of State because he thought the President's policies were leading to war. Until the last moment, Bryan spent day and night speaking against war. The more militant groups jeered and booed him, sometimes chanting, "We'll hang Bill Bryan to a sour apple tree." He was ridiculed, abused, branded a traitor and threatened with assassination, but still he kept up his antiwar plea.

However, once war actually came, Bryan joined with the rest of the country in supporting it. He even offered to enlist as a private, despite the fact that he was already sixty-five years old. Bryan was bowing to the popular will, which he thought was the right thing to do in a democracy. This belief made him intolerant of those who refused to fight, and he couldn't understand how anyone could be a conscientious objector.

But Oswald Garrison Villard's reaction to the American declaration of war was very different from Bryan's. "It came nearer to unmanning me than anything in my life," he said. "For I knew, as I knew that I lived, that this ended the Republic as we had known it; that henceforth we Americans were to be part and parcel of world politics, rivalries, jealousies, and militarism; that hate, prejudice and passion were now enthroned in the United States . . . The fundamental foreign policy of the Republic—to remain aloof from the jealousies, intrigues and wars of Europe—was thrown overboard."

7 War Hysteria

AMERICA, 1917—The streets of Bisbee, Arizona, were dark and empty at 6:30 on the morning of July 12. Normally the laborers in this small mining town would already be up and dressed, gulping the last of their morning coffee before heading for the copper mines.

But today everything was still, for the workers were on strike. They had forced the copper mines to shut down for more than two weeks.

The strike had been organized by the International Workers of the World (IWW)—also known as the Wobblies, and frequently jeered as the "I Won't Work-ers"— the most angry and radical of the labor groups. Although the IWW was not too strong anywhere except in the West, its militant tactics and lack of support for the war effort had inflamed America's temper—which, in these wartime days, was very short indeed.

Newspapers across the country villified the IWW as disloyal, unpatriotic traitors and saboteurs who were deliberately helping Germany by organizing strikes. Some even thought that the union's activities were financed by Germany. Hatred of this group was so intense that patriotic citizens had begun taking matters into their own hands.

On this particular morning in Bisbee, just before the sun broke over the horizon, bands of armed men suddenly appeared in the streets. One band emerged from an alley, while the others had been hiding in storerooms and darkened business offices. They fanned out across the workers' district, breaking into homes and dragging men out at gunpoint. Anyone who had any connection with the strike, or even sympathized with it, was seized by the gun-wielding vigilantes.

Within a few hours, 1186 workers had been rounded up and were being held captive in the Bisbee baseball park. Then they were marched to the railroad station and herded into cattle and freight cars. They stayed there for some time, jammed together without food or water, while the train rolled on to Columbus, New Mexico.

However, the people in Columbus refused to let the workers disembark in their town, so the vigilantes had to find another place to unload their human cargo. They decided on Hermanas, New Mexico, a small way station isolated in the middle of the flaming-hot desert. Here the workers were abandoned without provisions of any sort. Eventually the United States Army was called in to provide temporary shelter and food for the deported strikers.

This was just one of the countless cruel and lawless incidents that took place during the war years—all in the name of patriotism. The war produced such hysterical fervor among Americans that anyone who dared criticize the war or the Government was in danger of mob violence. (The full story of this persecution of antiwar dissenters was detailed by H. C. Peterson and Gilbert C. Fite in their book *Opponents of War, 1917–1918.*)

Since the more radical labor and political groups opposed the war as a "capitalistic" adventure, it became easy to attack and repress them for "disloyalty." The war provided a convenient excuse for clamping down on outspoken rebels who were bent on changing the economic or political status quo.

In the Bisbee incident, for example, the vigilante group included many officials of the mining companies, whose economic interests were threatened by the strikers. They claimed that the shutdown of the mines was hurting the war effort, but it was hurting their own pocketbooks as well. Their patriotic ardor just happened to coincide with their financial interest.

However, the times were such that Americans would tolerate almost anything that was done in the name of patriotism. The IWW was one of many radical groups that suffered greatly from the repressiveness of the war years, although no one—no matter how "respectable"—was safe to speak out against the war.

Shortly after America entered the fray, a large number of superpatriotic groups sprang up. Among them were the American Defense Society, the National Security League, the Knights of Liberty, the Anti-Yellow Dog League, and the Boy Spies of America. These were all private organizations, although they often worked hand in hand with the local police to silence any opposition to the war.

One of the most active of these groups was the American Defense Society. It had its own Vigilante Patrol, numbering hundreds of men, who prowled the streets in search of soapbox antiwar speakers. The Patrol captured its first victim on August 22, 1917, just five days after it had been organized.

The speaker, a man named Bedford, had been addressing a sidewalk crowd on Broadway and Thirty-seventh Street in New York City. The Vigilante Patrol accused him of saying that he did not approve of sending American troops to France to fight England's battles. For this treacherous statement, the Patrol had Bedford arrested and charged with disorderly conduct. The honorary president of the American Defense Society was Theodore Roosevelt, always a fighting man, and now one of the country's fiercest hawks.

Another, more frightening private patriotic group was the American Protective League, which had close links with the Department of Justice. By June 1917, the League had branches in 600 cities across the nation, and a membership of almost 100,000. Within another year, its membership swelled to 250,000 eager patriots, who spent their time ferreting out disloyal tendencies among their neighbors.

League members were the pillars of their communities —the bankers, the businessmen, and the industrial leaders. They did their work for the League with enthusiasm, exposing about three million cases of so-called disloyalty during the war years and afterwards.

Their activity alarmed Secretary of the Treasury William McAdoo, who thought it wrong that people should be able to obtain membership in the Protective League, for $.75 or $1, and have the authority, "with the approval of the Department of Justice, to make investigations under the title of 'Secret Service.'"

President Wilson also eyed the League nervously. In a memo to Attorney General Thomas Watt Gregory, he protested, "It seems to me that it would be very dangerous to have such an organization operating in the United States, and I wonder if there is any way in which we could stop it." However, the Attorney General continued to support the League, and the President took no further action.

Wilson had grimly foreseen what would happen once America entered the war. In the dark days leading up to the declaration against Germany, Wilson told the editor of the New York *World:* "Once lead this people into war and they'll forget there ever was such a thing as tolerance. To fight, you must be brutal and ruthless, and the spirit of ruthless brutality will enter into the very fiber of our national life, infecting Congress, the courts, the policeman on the beat, the man in the street."

But Wilson himself had to share some of the blame for this intolerance, for he did very little to stop it. Also, he had called upon Congress to pass laws that, in practice, virtually cut off the right of free speech in America. The two major laws that were used for this purpose were the Espionage Act of 1917 and the Sedition Act of 1918.

The Sedition Act, in particular, was very sweeping. It called for the punishment of anyone who in wartime "shall willfully utter, print, write, or publish any disloyal, profane, scurrilous, or abusive language about the form of government of the United States, or the Constitution of the United States, or the military or naval forces of the United States, or the flag of the United States, or the uniform of the Army or Navy," or use any language intended to bring these institutions "into contempt, scorn, contumely or disrepute."

It was also illegal to obstruct the sale of war bonds, interfere with the draft in any way, incite disloyalty, or advocate labor strikes in industries that were needed for war production. Furthermore, the Postmaster General could refuse to deliver any mail that he thought might be "objectionable" under the terms of the Espionage and Sedition acts. Because of this provision, antiwar or pacifist literature could not be sent through the mails.

During the raging Congressional debate over the Sedition Act, several senators came out flatly against it. Senator Thomas W. Hardwick "gagged" over it, warning that if it passed, "free speech in a free country will simply mean that one man is perfectly free to advocate war to the end of eternity and another man cannot advocate peace without putting himself in a dungeon."

Senator Hiram Johnson said that passing the bill would be like declaring "war on the American people . . . Measures such as this do not unite a people; they breed discontent; they cause suspicion to stalk all through the land; they make the one man the spy upon the other; they take a great, virile, brave people and make that people timid and fearful."

The Sedition Act was so broad that it could be used to stifle any criticism of the war or the Government whatsoever. When it was finally passed, the Milwaukee *Journal* advised its readers, "Your best course is not to talk about the war at all."

With laws like the Espionage and Sedition acts to support them, the prowar vigilante groups flourished. In Missouri, one group sent out "warning cards" to anyone who was heard mouthing antiwar remarks. A white warning card simply told the person he was being watched. This was enough to silence most people, but in some cases additional warnings were needed. These were sent on blue cards. If the accused still continued to express antiwar feelings, he was sent a red card informing him that he had been reported to the Secret Service.

Even children were recruited as eavesdroppers. The Anti-Yellow Dog League consisted of several thousand young detectives, age ten or more, who were supposed to be on the alert for antiwar comments.

There were many lynching cases during these years, as well as thousands of other acts of violence. People who refused to buy liberty bonds were tarred and feathered or strung from flagpoles. Others were painted yellow—the favorite color for "traitors" or "cowards." Still others were driven out of town on rails.

In March of 1918, a member of a patriotic group in Tulsa, Oklahoma, shot and killed a waiter in a restaurant who was accused of making pro-German remarks. At his trial, the patriot, S. L. Miller, was found "Not Guilty." The newspapers backed him all the way, with one of them noting afterward: "The decision was received with cheers, and men, women, and children rushed to Miller to congratulate him both for his patriotism and the outcome of the trial."

Even eminent public figures were in danger. Among the foremost peace advocates, both before and during the war, was Senator Robert M. LaFollette. As one of the most dynamic reformers of his time, LaFollette had waged many battles—for an eight-hour working day, a graduated income tax, public ownership of utilities, and government supervision of industry. But the crusade that gained him the most enemies was the one he waged against the war.

President Wilson blasted LaFollette as one of a "little group of willful men" who were trying to stop America from arming for battle. Afterward, LaFollette opposed the draft, fought the Espionage Act, and tried to impose heavy taxes on businessmen who were profiting from the war. This last effort failed dismally.

In September 1917, LaFollette made an antiwar speech that sent patriotic citizens into a rage. He implied that the Germans had good cause to sink the passenger ship *Lusitania* two years earlier because it was loaded with munitions, and that Americans should not have been traveling on a British liner in time of war.

Speaking off the cuff to a liberal Non-Partisan League crowd in Minnesota, LaFollette said:

Now, fellow citizens, we are in the midst of a war. For my own part I was not in favor of beginning the war. I don't mean to say that we hadn't suffered griev-ances; we had at the hands of Germany, serious griev-ances! We had cause for complaint. They had inter-fered with the right of American citizens to travel upon the high seas—on ships loaded with munitions for Great Britain. I say this, that the comparatively small privilege of the right of an American citizen to ride on a munition-loaded ship, flying a foreign flag, is too small to involve this Government in the loss of millions and millions of lives!

Four days before the *Lusitania* sailed, President Wil-son was warned in person by Secretary of State Bryan that the *Lusitania* had six million rounds of ammuni-tion aboard, besides explosives; and that the passengers who proposed to sail on that vessel were sailing in violation of a statute of this country . . .

In these days of 1917, with the flags all about us commemorating liberty—constitutional liberty—we are inhibited from even discussing this war, from even suggesting that there might be some way with honor and credit to our Government to terminate and stop the awful slaughter and the awful expense . . .

After this speech, cries of outrage echoed from coast to coast. The sinking of the *Lusitania* had become the nation's battle cry during the war, and anyone who cast doubts on America's righteousness in the affair could only be a traitor. Governor Burnquist of Minnesota said that he was launching an investigation immediately, and if LaFollette's speech was found to be seditious and disloyal, he would have the Senator arrested at once.

Theodore Roosevelt bellowed that LaFollette was "loyally and efficiently serving one country—Germany," while the Minneapolis *Tribune* denounced his speech as "treasonable."

There were cries from all quarters to have LaFollette expelled from the Senate, along with his antiwar cronies —Senators Stone, Gronna, Hardwick, Reed, and Vardmann. This little group was the nucleus of the peace faction in the Senate.

The move to oust LaFollette gained momentum, and within a short time the Senate began an investigation of its most controversial member. A special committee was formed to hear charges and gather evidence, but there was really nothing substantial against LaFollette. The committee could never prove that anything he had said in his speech was inaccurate.

Finally, in January 1919, after the war was over, the Senate voted to drop charges against LaFollette. This decision was made reluctantly, and one Senator was heard to grumble as he left the chamber, "Damn him anyway. He ought to be thrown out of the Senate. He is always against money."

As the war went on, persecution of groups opposed to the war reached a crescendo. The International Workers of the World (Wobblies) were all but wiped out by the joint efforts of the Government and private patriotic groups.

The Wobblies were mainly poor, unskilled, uneducated laborers who had no stake in American society. Discontented and prone to violence, they flung threats at the upper classes and vowed to overthrow the capitalist system. The only war they cared about was the class war between capital and labor. The worldwide conflict meant absolutely nothing to them, so they turned their backs on it.

As one Wobbly said when asked about his attitude toward the war:

If you were a bum without a blanket; if you had left your wife and kids when you went west for a job, and had never located them since; if your job had never kept you long enough in a place to qualify you to vote; if you slept in a lousy, sour bunkhouse, and ate food just as rotten as they could give you and get by with it; if deputy sheriffs shot your cooking cans full of holes and spilled your grub on the ground; if your wages were lowered on you when the bosses thought they had you down . . . if every person who represented law and order and the nation beat you up, railroaded you to jail, and the good Christian people cheered and told them to go to it, how in hell do you expect a man to be patriotic? This war is a businessman's war, and we don't see why we should go out and get shot in order to save the lovely state of affairs that we now enjoy.

Violence and sabotage were part of the Wobblies' revolutionary creed, but their actual use of violence never matched the violence that was done to them in return.

One of many bloody incidents involved a well-known Wobbly organizer, Frank Little. He was a small, intense man who was part Cherokee Indian. Despite being crippled and having only one eye, he dashed around the country from one labor uprising to another. He had been jailed and beaten many times, but this rarely slowed him for very long.

In the summer of 1917, Frank Little turned up in Butte, Montana, where the United Metal Mine Workers Union was striking. The strike came on the heels of a fire in the Anaconda Copper Mines that had killed 160 miners. Now the Union was demanding higher safety standards and better wages, among other things.

Fanning the unrest as much as he could, Little made several speeches in Butte, attacking the capitalists and criticizing the Government for having used troops to put down strikes. His speeches inflamed the business and professional leaders in Butte, who regarded him as a dangerous troublemaker.

At 3 A.M. on the morning of August 1, several men drove up to the boardinghouse where Little was staying. They banged on the door and woke the housekeeper, who let them in after they announced that they were police officers. Once inside, they crashed into Little's room, dragging him out of bed and forcing him into the car that was parked outside. Later, they tied him behind the car and dragged him through the streets of town until his knees were scaped to the bone. After reaching the outskirts of Butte, the men hung Little from a railroad trestle until he was dead. They left a note pinned to his shirt, reading, "Others take notice. First and last warning. 3-7-77." This was the sign of the frontier vigilantes.

More than 3000 miners attended Little's funeral, but the nation as a whole was not terribly upset by his death. Many solid citizens felt that he deserved it. Even the New York *Times* seemed to share this attitude. Although the *Times* called the lynching "deplorable and detestable," it also said that "the IWW agitators are in effect, and perhaps in fact, agents of Germany. The Federal authorities should make short work of these treasonable conspirators against the United States."

Only a minority of the press seemed to feel that there was another side to the story. As the Macon *Telegraph* noted, "We suspect that outraged patriotism had mighty little to do with the lynching of Frank Little out in Butte, but we do suspect that certain influences very much opposed to strikes in general and strikes for higher wages in particular might have had a fairly efficient left-handed part in it."

When a Wobbly in Bingham, Utah, was heard to curse the United States Government and damn the flag, he was arrested by National Guardsmen and received a bayonet wound in his back. Another Wobbly in Franklin, New Jersey, was nearly lynched by the chief of police and a group of businessmen. However, at the last moment, when he was unconscious and near death, they cut him down and took him to jail instead. He received a three-month sentence.

The Wobblies were so closely linked in the public's mind to spies, traitors, saboteurs, and pro-Germans that "respectable" people could do anything to them and get away with it. When four Wobblies in Arkansas tried to organize black workers in the rice fields, and demanded a five-dollar-a-day minimum wage for them, the landowners sprang into action.

First, they had the Wobblies arrested for disturbing the peace. Then, one night 150 armed men showed up at the jail, snatched the four prisoners and took them to an isolated area. After brutally whipping their captives, they poured boiling hot tar on their naked, bleeding bodies, and then applied a coat of feathers. In this wretched condition, the Wobblies were driven from the area and warned that if they ever came back they would be lynched.

The Government, too, regarded the Wobblies as a dangerous element. In a sudden, startling raid on September 5, 1917, Federal agents swooped down on IWW headquarters in thirty-three different cities. They seized files, books, newspapers, pamphlets, letters, account books, and even a batch of love letters. Private homes were also raided, as a giant dragnet was thrown over the Wobblies from coast to coast. More raids followed during the next few weeks, until the Government had amassed five tons of materials belonging to the organization.

On September 28, 166 officers and workers of the IWW were indicted—primarily for conspiracy against the United States war program. The Wobblies were accused of conspiring to obstruct, hinder, and delay by strikes and acts of violence the production and transportation of war supplies. They were also charged with obstructing the draft, urging soldiers to desert, and conspiring to commit thousands of war-related offenses against the United States.

A mass trial was set for the following spring in Chicago. Meanwhile, Federal agents had to sift through the tons of seized material in search of concrete evidence that could be used against the Wobblies.

By the time the trial began, charges against 53 of the defendants had been dropped. The remaining 113 Wobblies took their places in the Chicago courtroom on May 1, 1918. The best-known of the defendants was William (Big Bill) Haywood, head of the IWW.

A large, square-faced man with a scar over one eye and a flattened nose that had taken too many punches, Bill Haywood looked the part of a brawling laborer. He had always denied that the Wobblies were trying to obstruct the war effort. Although they were against the war, he said, the purpose of their strikes was not to hurt war production.

"We are not thinking of the war at all in these strikes," he once said. "In that respect, we don't know there's a war. What we are doing is trying to improve the conditions of our boys—their living and working conditions. If it is to their advantage to call a strike now, they will call it without any regard to the war."

Nevertheless, the Government played up the Union's antiwar attitude throughout the trial. Testimony that the Wobblies had burned and destroyed machinery during strikes was seen as evidence of sabotage, aimed at hampering the war effort. Although the Wobblies insisted that such tactics were meant to coerce employers, and had nothing to do with the war, the Government hammered away at the "sabotage" issue.

On August 30, after deliberating for less than an hour, the jury handed in a verdict of "guilty" for 96 of the defendants. Big Bill Haywood was shocked, for as he saw it, there was no proof of actual sabotage against him or his men. "I can't understand how some of us were not acquitted at a moment's notice," he said afterward.

Haywood was even more shocked at his sentence—twenty years in jail and a $30,000 fine. The other defendants received sentences ranging from one to fifteen years.

Two other mass trials of the IWW followed—one in Sacramento, California, the other in Kansas City, Kansas. The charges against the Wobblies were similar in both cases, and so were the verdicts. In Sacramento, all 46 defendants were found guilty; in Kansas City, 26 Wobblies were convicted.

All in all, the three mass trials resulted in the conviction of 168 members of the IWW. It seemed as if the organization itself was on trial, rather than individuals, and the crackdown effectively crushed the labor group.

While most of the nation rejoiced, there were some lonely voices who insisted that the Wobblies had been ill-treated. Among them was the National Civil Liberties Bureau, an offshoot of the American Union Against Militarism. The Bureau had been formed in 1917 to protect the basic rights of those who opposed the war, particularly conscientious objectors. Its founder was Roger Baldwin, and its members included Norman Thomas and Oswald Garrison Villard, plus other pacifists, social workers, and socialists. Some of the most prominent peace workers, such as Lillian Wald and Jane Addams, didn't want to be connected with the Bureau because they felt it was pitting itself against the Government in time of war.

Shortly before the Wobblies went on trial in Chicago, the Civil Liberties Bureau came out with a highly controversial pamphlet, *The Truth About the IWW*. This was practically the only nonlabor publication that defended the Wobblies, saying that they had not obstructed the war nor advocated violence, disloyalty, treason, or pro-Germanism.

The Bureau took the position that the IWW was a legitimate labor organization whose motives were economic and not political. It also pointed out that the Wobblies had been directly responsible for only 3 of 521 labor disputes that had taken place between April and October 1917. By bringing the IWW leaders to trial, the pamphlet concluded, the Government was trying to crush a legitimate labor group.

The Government was incensed by the pamphlet, and immediately took steps to suppress it. The Post Office declared it nonmailable, and the Justice Department asked express companies not to carry it. Although the pamphlet did create a stir, its major effect was to create some very powerful enemies for the Civil Liberties Bureau.

Roger Baldwin had anticipated such difficulties when he first set up the Bureau, but his own deep-rooted pacifism prompted him to do all he could for other war opponents. Primarily, he wanted the Government to broaden the basis for draft exemptions, but it was a futile battle.

Throughout the war, the Government would only exempt members of "well-recognized" religious sects that forbid their members to participate in war "in any form."

Practically the only ones who qualified under this ruling were Quakers and Mennonites. Members of smaller, more obscure religious sects wound up in jail if they refused to serve in the Army. Pacifists, socialists, and others who were against the war for moral or political reasons also spent time in jail.

Although the Civil Liberties Bureau could not help these men get exemptions, it did try to improve the harsh conditions under which they lived in the jailhouses and detention camps. As in the country at large, the jailed war opponents were treated like the worst type of criminals. The guards beat and abused them, and even the other prisoners looked down on them. Practically the only group they could turn to for help was the Civil Liberties Bureau.

Roger Baldwin himself spent time in jail as a conscientious objector. Although he was a member of a wealthy New England family that traced its ancestry back to the *Mayflower*, he was really not as much of a rebel as one might think. His father and grandfather had long been active in liberal and reform crusades, and he was simply carrying on the family tradition. But as one writer noted, he carried it so far that he broke it.

After emerging from jail, he remarked that his experience had not been wholly bad. "I am a graduate of Harvard," he told reporters, "but a year in jail has helped me to recover from it."

After the war ended, Baldwin reorganized the Bureau into the American Civil Liberties Union (ACLU). This group was not concerned solely with pacifism, but with preserving and protecting the Bill of Rights in a nation that had grown dangerously intolerant of dissent. Today, the ACLU is the largest and most powerful civil liberties group in America.

Another group that suffered greatly during the war years were the Socialists. They had never tried to hide their bitter antiwar feelings. The day after America declared war on Germany, the Socialist leaders held an emergency meeting in St. Louis. They passed a series of very strong antiwar resolutions that were supported by the more radical members of the Party. But other Socialists refused to oppose the war, so the resolutions caused a deep rift in the Party. The resolutions said in part:

The Socialist Party of the United States in the present grave crisis solemnly reaffirms its allegiance to the principle of internationalism and working-class solidarity the world over and proclaims its unalterable opposition to the war just declared by the Government of the United States.

Modern wars as a rule have been caused by the commercial and financial rivalry and intrigues of the capitalist interests in the different countries. Whether they have been frankly waged as wars of aggression or have been hypocritically represented as wars of "defense," they have always been made by the classes and fought by the masses. War brings wealth and power to the ruling classes and suffering, death and demoralization to the workers.

. . . We, therefore, call upon the workers of all countries to refuse to support their governments in their wars. The wars of the contending national groups of capitalists are not the concern of the workers. The only struggle which would justify the workers in taking up arms is the great struggle of the working class of the world to free itself from economic exploitation and political oppression. As against the false doctrine of national patriotism, we uphold the ideal of international working-class solidarity . . .

The Socialist resolution didn't go over too well with the American people, who were just beginning to whip themselves into a prowar frenzy. However, serious attacks against the Party didn't really begin until seven months later, when the American people were horrified to learn that the Communists had seized control of Russia.

Americans had never seen much difference between Socialists and Communists; all radicals seemed pretty much alike to them. In confusing other left-wing groups with the feared and hated Communists, Americans cracked down hard on the Socialist Party.

Socialist candidates for office were denounced as traitors. The state chairman of the South Dakota Socialist Party was arrested on a technical charge of "desertion" after he registered as a conscientious objector. He was sentenced to twenty years in the penitentiary. When the Party tried to hold its annual state convention in Mitchell, South Dakota, the police broke up the meeting.

A Nevada Socialist who was nearly elected to office was fired by his employer and then arrested for making seditious remarks. He was accused of saying that the worldwide conflict was nothing but a capitalistic war, and if it was not for the "graft and money to be made by the capitalists, the United States would never have gone into war." He was fined $300 and sentenced to two years in prison.

Socialist Anna Blachly of Klamath Falls, Oregon, a

housewife with two children, was forced to buy war bonds by local patriots. They told her that if she refused, she would be hung by the neck. Afterward, the local vigilante group ordered all Socialists to leave town. Mrs. Blachly fled to Portland, Oregon, where she felt that people were less "barbarous."

The Government, too, joined the attack against the Socialists. During the summer of 1917, the *American Socialist* newspaper was barred from the mails. Immediately following this, sixty Socialist newspapers were deprived of their second-class mailing rights, without which no newspaper could survive.

In September, one of the most important Socialist publications—the Milwaukee *Leader*—lost its mailing privileges. President Wilson didn't think it was either wise or fair to suppress the *Leader*. After the hearing, in which the verdict went against the newspaper, the President wrote to the Postmaster General saying: "I am afraid you will be shocked, but I must say that I do not find this hearing very convincing. Some of the things quoted probably cross the line, and I have very little doubt that they were all intended to have sinister results, but I must frankly say that I do not think that most of what is quoted ought to be regarded as unmailable." The President's mild protest was safely ignored, and the Milwaukee *Leader* lost a great many of its subscribers.

The editor of the *Leader* was Victor Berger, an Austrian immigrant who had come to the United States in 1878 and helped organize the Socialist Party. Milwaukee was a Socialist stronghold, and in 1911 Berger became the first Socialist member of Congress.

A mild-looking man with a white, bristly mustache and round, gold-rimmed glasses, Berger wrote many strident editorials against the war, and was one of the nation's most vocal antiwar spokesmen.

In 1918, while campaigning as the Socialist candidate for the United States Senate, Berger was suddenly indicted for violating the Espionage Act. However, he continued to campaign, and polled over 100,000 votes in defeat.

Berger was brought to trial together with four other Socialists, who were charged with conspiracy in writing and circulating pro-German literature. Presiding over the Chicago courtroom was Judge Kenesaw Landis—a man well-known for his hatred of Socialists.

The verdict was "Guilty," and Judge Landis sentenced each of the men to twenty years in prison. Berger protested that it was a "political" trial, and that he and the others had been convicted just for teaching socialism. "The Socialist Party was on trial," he declared.

The decision was appealed to the United States Supreme Court, which ruled in 1921 that the Socialists' original request to be tried by a different judge than Landis should have been granted. On these grounds, the High Court dismissed the case.

However, even before the original trial began, Berger was elected to the House of Representatives. His fellow Congressmen couldn't tolerate such an upstart in their midst, and on November 10, 1919, they voted against seating him. There was only one vote in his favor.

Berger ran for the same post again in a special election, and again he won—and again the House refused to seat him. In 1922, Berger was elected for a third time. By now, the intense hostility against Socialists had subsided somewhat, so that Berger was able to take his rightful place in Congress.

The suppression of Socialist newspapers and the conviction of Berger and other leading Party members weakened the Socialists considerably. But the biggest blow was the arrest and conviction of their charismatic leader, Eugene V. Debs.

A labor leader turned Socialist, Debs had deep, intense feelings for the workingman. As a youth, he had been a fireman on the Terre Haute and Indianapolis Railway. He organized his fellow workers into a union in 1875, and by 1893 he founded and led the American Railway Union. A year later he called a strike against the Chicago Pullman Company, which turned out to be one of the wildest episodes in labor history. Federal troops were called in to subdue the rioting, and Debs was sent to jail for six months.

Debs had always been a man of action, a superb speaker and agitator, but never much of an intellectual. In jail, however, he became absorbed in the writings of Karl Marx, and by the time he was released, he was a socialist. In 1897 he founded the Social Democratic Party of America, which soon became the Socialist Party of America.

By 1912, Debs had run for President on the Socialist ticket four consecutive times. He had a large and loyal personal following, for a great many people were drawn by his unassuming charm and warmth. Some thought of him as a saintlike figure, a man they could worship as well as vote for.

Debs was as strongly opposed to the war as the other top Socialists in the country, but while they were speaking their minds and going to jail for it, he was strangely hesitant. By the early spring of 1918, he was one of the few Socialist leaders who was not yet on trial or behind bars, for he had not really taken a major part in the antiwar movement. Also, the Government was reluctant to act against him because of his intensely loyal mass following.

However, as Debs saw more and more of his fellow Socialists being thrown into prison, he grew increasingly militant in his attacks on the Government and the war. By the summer, he was ready to abandon all caution, and confront the Federal authorities head on.

To publicize his antiwar stand and arouse the people, Debs decided to deliberately provoke the Government into acting against him. He made his stand at Canton, Ohio, before the statewide Socialist convention. In a rousing, fierce antiwar speech, Debs said many things that he knew would be punishable under the Espionage and Sedition acts.

He told his audience, "You need to know that you are fit for something better than slavery and cannon fodder." He attacked Wall Street businessmen, the press, the clergy, the Supreme Court and high government officials. For the Communists, he had only praise. "Here, in this alert and inspiring assemblage our hearts are with the Bolsheviki of Russia," he said.

Throughout the speech, Debs repeatedly expressed sympathy for all the antiwar people who had been jailed, particularly his fellow Socialist Rose Pastor Stokes. Mrs. Stokes had said that she did not support the United States Government in the war. "No government which is for the profiteers can also be for the people," she had stated, "and I am for the people while the Government is for the profiteers."

In commenting on Mrs. Stokes' conviction, Debs remarked:

> Why the other day they sent a woman to Wichita Penitentiary for ten years. Just think of sentencing a woman to the penitentiary for talking! . . . The United States under the rule of the plutocrats is the only country which would send a woman to the penitentiary for ten years for exercising the right of free speech. If this be treason, let them make the most of it.

"They" certainly did make the most of it. A government stenographer had been in the audience while Debs spoke, taking down every word he said. Within two weeks, Debs was indicted for violating the Espionage Act—specifically, for having encouraged resistance to the United States; having tried to incite insubordination, disloyalty, and mutiny in the armed forces; and having obstructed recruiting.

At his trial, Debs freely admitted saying all the things he was accused of saying—and added that he would not retract a single word. "I have been accused of having obstructed the war," he said. "I admit it. Gentlemen, I abhor war."

He was sentenced to prison for ten years. On appeal, the Supreme Court rejected Debs's plea that he was exercising his right of free speech. His antiwar talk, the Court said, presented a "clear and present danger" to the nation.

Debs's conviction rocked the Socialist Party, and upset many other people who admired Debs without necessarily sharing his political views.

After the war ended, there was strong public pressure

on President Wilson to pardon Debs. The Government was bombarded with letters, protests, and petitions for Debs's release, as well as for a general amnesty for all political prisoners.

After a while, word reached Debs that a pardon might be granted if only he would repent. Upon hearing this, Debs exploded:

Repent! Repent! Repent for standing like a man! For having a conviction about a public question, and standing by it for the cause! Why, before I would don the sackcloth and get down into the ashes before the Attorney General or any other man on earth for having a principle, I would gladly walk to the gallows or the stake!

The appeals for his release continued without letup. Typical of the pleas was one from Oswald Garrison Villard, who wrote to Secretary of State Robert Lansing:

I wonder whether you can privately hold out any hope for the early release of Eugene Debs? You were good enough to say to me in Paris that you thought he ought to be released and would be as soon as he had served a little while.

I am wondering whether the Cabinet has any conception of the tremendous feeling of bitterness throughout the country among people who have never known Mr. Debs, and who, like myself, have never even heard him speak and do not belong to his Socialist Party. I think it would do much to allay the prevailing unrest . . . if he and other political prisoners like Kate

Richards O'Hare who are in prison solely because of their opinions, were released.

But when President Wilson was urged by some of his advisers to release the Socialist leader, he flatly refused. He said he would never consent to Debs's pardon, because the man was "a traitor to his country."

Wilson's successor, Warren G. Harding, took a much less harsh view of Debs. On Christmas Day, 1921, Harding had Debs released from Atlanta prison. When Debs returned to his home in Terre Haute, Indiana, jubilant crowds of more than 25,000 admirers were waiting to greet him.

The Debs case was by far the biggest *cause célèbre* among antiwar groups. But there were thousands of cases of intolerance and repression involving ordinary people, whom the public never knew of or heard about. Aliens —whether they supported the war or not—were frequently persecuted and suspected of being enemy spies. Anyone with a foreign accent came under suspicion.

For many newly arrived immigrants from the "wrong" countries, the war years were agony. They still had attachments to their native lands—with friends and family living there—but all at once their new homeland was at war with the old. Young men who still had fond memories of growing up in Germany, Austria, or elsewhere were now expected to don American uniforms and kill their former countrymen. Many were able to do this, but those who were not went to jail for refusing to fight. As Jane Addams remarked, the war was "exquisite torture" for them.

Even after the war, the persecution did not stop. Early

in 1920, thousands of radicals—Communists, anarchists, Wobblies and others—were seized during a series of raids led by Attorney General A. Mitchell Palmer. The Palmer raids were sparked by hysterical false fears that Communists were taking over America, just as they had taken over Russia. Hundreds of aliens who were captured in Palmer's dragnet were swiftly deported to their native lands.

The Palmer raids were a tragic but predictable climax to an era of rising intolerance. The repressive measures that had first been used to silence war opponents were also conveniently available for use against labor agitators, political rebels, aliens, and others who didn't conform to "the American way."

8 Between Two Wars

AMERICANS HAD PLUNGED into the Great War with absolute faith that they were making the world "safe for democracy" (and blind to the fact that they were losing it at home). The war was supposed to put an end to all wars, and to establish a new world order based on ideals of fairness and justice.

Disillusionment came quickly. By the time the Paris Peace Conference was over, Americans were not so sure that the war had really changed anything. Within fifteen years, most would probably have agreed with William Allen White, editor of a Kansas newspaper, who wrote in 1933:

> Fifteen years ago came the Armistice and we all thought it was to be a new world. It is! But a lot worse than it was before.
>
> Ten million men were killed and many more maimed, fifty billion dollars' worth of property destroyed, the world saddled with debts.
>
> And for what? Would it have been any worse if

Germany had won? Ask yourself honestly. No one knows.

. . . The boys who died just went out and died. To their own souls' glory, of course—but what else? . . . Yet the next war will see the same hurrah and the same bowwow of the big dogs to get the little dogs to go out and follow the blood scent and get their entrails tangled in the barbed wire.

And for what?

War is the devil's joke on humanity.

The seeds of another world war were planted in the treaty that ended the first one, although few people could have predicted this at the time.

President Woodrow Wilson had gone to Paris with visions of setting up a just and lasting peace, based on his fourteen points. These included "open covenants openly arrived at" (meaning no secret treaties to carve up the world); freedom of the seas to safeguard the rights of neutrals and small nations; the removal of economic barriers; equality of trade; the reduction of armaments by all nations; and a fair adjustment of colonial claims. But by far the most important item in Wilson's mind was the fourteenth point—the creation of a League of Nations to maintain everlasting peace.

When he arrived in Europe, millions of people lined the streets to cheer him. He was regarded almost as a "messiah," an apostle of peace who would finally bring an end to the bloody, drawn-out siege.

But the people's adoration of Wilson was not shared by their leaders. Lloyd George of England, Georges Clemenceau of France, and Vittorio Orlando of Italy—three of the "big four" who drew up the Versailles Treaty

—were snidely contemptuous of Wilson. They disliked his moral self-rightousness, and thought him naïve and ignorant about European affairs. Also, he was far too overbearing in the subtle game of diplomacy, so they were able to outmaneuver him easily.

The European leaders were not idealistic men. They were hard-nosed politicians, skilled in the international contests of intrigue, barter, and double-dealing. They were determined to squash Germany once and for all, and to advance their own nations' ambitions any way they could. Wilson's dream of a League of Nations meant little to them, but they used it as bait to force Wilson to water down most of his other fourteen points.

Right from the start they abandoned the idea of open covenants. Secret territorial agreements had been made even before the Peace Conference began, as well as promises to neutral nations to induce them to enter the war. These secret agreements conflicted with many of Wilson's fourteen points, and the disputes had to be thrashed out in private. For this reason, most conference sessions were held behind closed doors.

Newspapermen were outraged by this turn of events. After being denied entry to the opening meeting, reporter William Allen White remarked: "That settles it. That finishes the conference and Wilson. Lloyd George and Clemenceau will now take him upstairs into a private bedroom and fool him to death."

Thus, the first of Wilson's fourteen points, "open covenants openly arrived at," came to a swift end. As Clemenceau snorted from behind his magnificent white walrus mustache, "Mr. Wilson bores me with his fourteen points; why, God almighty has only ten." And Lloyd

George remarked, "If you want to succeed in politics, you must keep your conscience well under control."

The three European leaders didn't get along very well with each other, either. As the Peace Conference dragged on, meetings were torn apart by furious arguments and nasty political wrangling. Lloyd George and Clemenceau almost came to blows at one point, and Wilson had to step in to break it up. Vittorio Orlando withdrew from the conference temporarily after a dispute with Wilson, and the American President once threatened to do the same after another fierce argument. By the time the Peace Conference was over, it was fortunate that the Allies were not at war with each other.

President Wilson returned to the United States with a peace treaty far different than the one he had envisioned. It was extremely harsh and vindictive. The Allied Powers had swooped down on Germany like a pack of greedy vultures, and all that was left was the bare skeleton of a once powerful nation. France, in particular, wanted to permanently cripple Germany so it could never again threaten France's military or economic security.

Germany was stripped of much of her territory and people, half her coal supply, and three quarters of her iron ore. Germany's industrially rich Saar Basin was put under French control for fifteen years, and Alsace-Lorraine was returned to France. Two small strips of German land went to Belgium, and northern Schleswig went to the Danes. The new nation of Poland was given a chunk of Germany's eastern frontier, and East Prussia was cut off from the rest of Germany by the newly carved Polish Corridor, which gave Poland "free and secure access to the sea."

The German colonies in Africa—including Southwest

Africa, Tanganyika, Togoland, Ruanda-Urundi and the Cameroons—were divided among Great Britain, France, and Belgium under a League of Nations mandate system. The German-owned islands in the Pacific, such as West Samoa, Nauru, New Guinea, and the North Pacific islands were also turned into League mandates, under the control of Japan, Australia, and New Zealand.

Germany's entire military and naval establishment was dismantled. In addition, Germany was ordered to pay reparations for the cost of the war, amounting to more than $56 billion, even though she had practically no resources left.

The Versailles Treaty was not an "agreement" on the terms of peace, since Germany and Austria had no voice in it at all. It was a punishment meted out by the victors to the losers—and the losers were forced to accept it *for the time being*.

Wilson admitted the treaty was severe, "but not unjust," he said. He backed the agreement because it contained the one thing he wanted most—a provision for a League of Nations. Wilson had sacrificed almost all his other goals in order to salvage this one, but by the time he got back home, the forces lined up against the League had grown very powerful.

Although the Democrats in the Senate supported the League and the treaty, they were no longer in the majority. In the elections of 1918, just before the Armistice, the Republicans had swept both houses of Congress. This was a direct slap at Wilson, stemming from the public's dislike of his dictatorial methods, plus weariness of wartime controls.

The new Republican majority in the Senate was against Wilson's Versailles package. There were many reasons for this, including party politics and personal animosities, but the general feeling was that America should not get too closely tied up with Europe and its problems now that the war was over. Nor did they want European nations to meddle in American affairs.

Some of these fears were shared by liberals and pacifists outside the Senate. They disliked the idea that America might be called upon to defend nations that were attacked, thereby sucking this country into other wars. Pacifists had long dreamed of a world congress that would iron out disputes by arbitration and conciliation —not by the threat of force. Although the League had many provisions that pacifists liked—such as a Permanent Court of International Justice—they were too afraid of the League's warlike teeth to support it all the way. Equally important, many liberals disliked the peace treaty to which the League was tied. Part of the League's job was to enforce the terms of the treaty, but opponents felt that these terms were too vindictive and selfish to settle anything for very long.

The fight against American entry into the League of Nations found many pacifists and liberals lined up alongside their old conservative foes. As Oswald Garrison Villard wrote:

It was hard for us to oppose the League, for all of us had dreamed of a parliament of man, and still harder to find ourselves fighting alongside of Boies Penrose and Henry Cabot Lodge and his satellites, but fight we did and so gave aid and comfort to those whom we opposed at every other point, whose whole influence upon our public life and social and economic

progress seemed to us about the most dangerous in our
politics. That had happened to us before and happened
to us again; one can only stick to the chart one has
chosen to sail by and not be diverted by the character
of the consorts that may for a brief moment take a
parallel course.

The Senate never ratified the Treaty of Versailles, nor
did America ever join the League of Nations. On May
20, 1920, Congress passed a joint resolution declaring the
war with Germany over. President Wilson vetoed it, but
it was passed again in July 1921, after Warren G. Harding had become President. After that, the United States
negotiated separate peace treaties with Germany, Austria,
and Hungary, all of which were ratified by the Senate.

Once disillusionment about the Great War set in, Americans recoiled from the notion of ever going to battle
again. They thought that the best way to guarantee
peace for themselves was to stay out of the League of
Nations; peace through isolation was their aim.

During these postwar years, the American peace movement flourished as never before. All shades and varieties
of peace groups sprang up, and those that had existed
earlier swelled to many times their former size.

Just as in previous eras, the peace movement was
divided along radical and conservative lines. The radicals
were actually "pacifists" in the more personal and absolute
sense, while the conservatives were simply people who
wanted to work for world peace.

Among the conservative groups was the Carnegie En-
dowment for International Peace, set up in 1910 by the

steel magnate Andrew Carnegie. He put $10 million into his group just for a start, to "hasten the abolition of international war."

Carnegie was cheerfully optimistic that all war would be banished from the earth in a short time, and afterward his organization could turn its energies to "the next most degrading evil." However, after more than sixty years of tireless activity, the organization is still working to end war.

Another wealthy, well-connected organization was the World Peace Foundation, also founded in 1910. The Woodrow Wilson Foundation, the Church Peace Union, and the League of Nations Association were similar, well-run conservative peace groups. A giant women's organization of this type was the National Committee on the Cause and Cure of War, which represented about six million women.

All these groups worked through established channels to educate the public, promote international good will, sponsor research, and strengthen the legal and judicial machinery for settling international disputes. In the belief that lasting peace demanded international cooperation, they never favored isolationism.

Among their major projects was a campaign to end military training in schools and colleges, and to do away with militarism altogether. These groups waged an all-out effort to prevent the outbreak of war with Mexico in 1924, and to put a stop to American meddling in China.

They also jumped into the battle to banish war by means of treaties, although this idea was really the brainchild of the American Committee for Outlawry of War. The Committee had been organized in 1921 by Solomon O. Levinson, a wealthy Chicago lawyer. He found a powerful ally for his cause in Senator William Borah, Chairman of the Senate Committee on Foreign Relations.

By 1927, the idea of outlawing war had become very popular in America, largely because of the propagandizing and agitation of all the peace groups. It seemed like such a clear-cut solution to an agonizing problem, and people were sure it would work if only nations would trust one another.

When the French Foreign Minister Anatole Briand suggested the idea of a pact to outlaw war between France and the United States, the American Secretary of State Frank Kellogg came out with a proposal for *all* nations to sign such an agreement.

The resulting Kellogg-Briand Pact was a spectacular triumph for all the peace groups. A total of sixty-two nations pledged to renounce war as an instrument of national policy, and for a brief while it really seemed as if there would be no more armed conflicts. But there was no way of enforcing the pact; it depended on mutual good will, which soon began to fade away.

Meanwhile, other efforts were underway to make war *unconstitutional* in the United States. A group called the Women's Peace Union sponsored a constitutional amendment saying in part, "War for any purpose shall be illegal . . . nor shall any funds be issued, appropriated or expended for such purpose."

This didn't appeal very much to most Americans, but it did gain the support of the more radical peace groups. Among them was the Women's International League for Peace and Freedom, the group that had been founded by Jane Addams in 1915. She still led the organization, which had 50,000 members in twenty-five different countries. The American branch alone numbered about

12,000, and was one of the most important peace groups in this country. In 1931, Jane Addams received the Nobel Peace Prize.

Other groups that backed the idea of an antiwar amendment included the Fellowship of Reconciliation, the National Council for Prevention of War, the War Resisters' League, the Women's Peace Society, and the Peace Section of the American Friends Service Committee.

All these groups were considered "radical" in that most of their members were actual pacifists who would not personally take part in any war. They were "war resisters," while members of the more conservative peace societies didn't take such an extreme stand. Also, the radical peace groups swung toward isolationism, particularly after 1930, while the conservative groups did not.

Most of the radical peace groups never grew very large, nor did they attract much popular support. Americans still thought of pacifists as those "cowards and traitors" who had refused to fight in the World War. Ironically, even though America was all for peace now, it was still highly prejudiced against absolute pacifists.

In fact, the lingering hostility to pacifists was so strong that they were no longer allowed to become American citizens. Under the laws of the 1920s, any alien who wanted to become a citizen had to take an oath swearing to support and defend the Constitution and laws of the United States against all enemies, and to *bear arms* for America when required by law. Pacifists who could not take this oath were denied citizenship, whether they were religious pacifists such as Quakers and Mennonites, or philosophical pacifists.

This was a new phase in American history, for in previous times pacifists had been as welcome as any other would-be citizens, at least in a legal sense. At times, the United States Government had even gone out of its way to attract pacifists to this country. For example, when it became known that a large group of Mennonites was planning to leave Russia in the 1870s, both Canada and the United States competed for them. Government officials helped them look for land, and President Ulysses S. Grant promised that if there was ever a war in which men were being drafted, Congress would free them "from duties which are asked of other citizens."

Despite their pacifism, the Mennonites had been regarded as highly desirable settlers because they were moral, industrious, sober, and frugal. As a senator from Nebraska said at the time, "In God's name, have we not enough of the fighting element in America? . . . Our people are a peculiar people; and if there is any portion of the world that can send us a few advocates of peace, in God's name let us bid them welcome. We want settlers of that kind."

But by the 1920s, Americans no longer felt that way. Pacifists who applied for citizenship were repeatedly turned down, even if they were women who would never even be asked to bear arms for their country.

One of the most celebrated legal cases of this time involved the pacifist writer and lecturer Rosika Schwimmer. Madame Schwimmer was born in Hungary, and had become one of the top political figures there. For a brief time she was a cabinet member in Hungary's moderate republican government, which was ousted by a communist takeover in 1919. At this point, Madame Schwimmer left Hungary and renounced her Hungarian citizenship, making her a woman without a country. For a time she lived in the United States as a resident alien, and then applied for American citizenship.

But Madame Schwimmer's pacifist views were well-known. She had been one of the leaders of Henry Ford's ill-starred Peace Voyage in 1915, and had lectured on pacifism throughout the country. Even though she was a woman in her middle fifties who could never be drafted into the Army, her pacifism was a barrier to citizenship.

At her hearing, the judge quizzed her repeatedly about her beliefs, asking her such questions as, "Would you kill someone who was about to take the life of an American soldier?"

She explained that she would do whatever she could to save the soldier, such as knocking the gun out of the assailant's hand, or sacrificing herself—but she could not kill. Even if her own life was at stake, she said, "I would not defend myself. I mean I wouldn't take a pistol to defend myself even if you handed it to me, under no circumstances."

Her application for citizenship was turned down. With the help of the newly formed American Civil Liberties Union, she took the case all the way up to the Supreme Court, but it was no use. The Court did not feel that pacifists necessarily had a right to become citizens.

This view prevailed until 1952, when Congress finally decreed that religious pacifists who wanted to become citizens did not have to take an oath to bear arms. Instead, they could promise to perform noncombatant service in the armed forces, or other work of "national importance." However, this would not have applied to

Madame Schwimmer, because she was a moral pacifist, not a religious one.

Even though many Americans could not forgive pacifists for refusing to fight in World War I, they themselves developed an intense hatred of war during the 1920s and 1930s. Books showing the futility and horror of war—such as Erich Maria Remarque's *All Quiet on the Western Front,* Ernest Hemingway's *A Farewell to Arms,* Laurence Stallings and Maxwell Anderson's *What Price Glory?* and John Dos Passos' *Three Soldiers*—made a smashing impact on the American people.

To add to the disillusionment about the Great War, a number of books came out charging that the munitions-makers had started it all, strictly for the profits. In *Merchants of Death,* the authors warned that the arms-makers had grown so powerful that they were one of the most dangerous factors in world politics—hindering peace and promoting war.

The peace groups demanded an investigation into the munitions industry, and largely through their efforts the Nye Committee was set up to scrutinize the arms trade. It found little concrete evidence of wrongdoing, although it did come up with some distasteful tidbits, such as the following note from an official of the Remington Arms Company:

The Paraguay and Bolivia fracas appears to be coming to a termination, so business from that end is probably finished. We certainly are in one hell of a business, where a fellow has to wish for trouble so as to make a living, the only consolation being, however, that if we don't get the business, someone else will.

It would be a terrible state of affairs if my conscience started to bother me now.

The Nye Committee also looked into charges that Wall Street tycoons had been responsible for getting the United States into war. The Committee put J. P. Morgan and Co. under a public microscope, but nothing much came out of this investigation either. The causes of the war were just too complex to be blamed only on the profit-makers.

Meanwhile, war clouds were already looming over the horizon. In 1931, the Japanese suddenly invaded Manchuria, dashing the dreams of those who thought that war was a thing of the past. The United States raged at this violation of the Kellogg-Briand Pact, which had flatly outlawed all war. The League of Nations looked into the matter, but did nothing.

Not long after this, Adolf Hitler's storm troopers began goose-stepping through the streets of Germany, while the Nazi Government quietly rearmed in violation of the Versailles Treaty. In 1935, Italy invaded Ethiopia. Despite Emperor Haile Selassie's desperate plea for help from the League of Nations, the League only applied half-hearted sanctions, which failed dismally. The following year, Germany openly remilitarized the Rhineland, and the League's disarmament talks collapsed.

The events in Europe made Americans want to retreat even further into their isolationist shell. Students held mass antiwar demonstrations, and as fears of war grew, they went on strike for peace. In April 1936, about 750,000 students in colleges across the country marched out of their classrooms to parade for peace. Professors who favored intervention in Europe's affairs were picketed by students wearing gas masks. In some cases, the students pinned toy medals on the professors. One startling poll, in which 21,725 college students were queried, showed that 39 percent of them were "uncompromising pacifists."

Although for the most part the students were deadly serious in their antiwar activities, there were some lighter touches to the student peace movement.

One student group—called the Veterans of Future Wars —was started as a practical joke among Princeton students, but the idea spread rapidly to about three hundred other campuses. The Future Veterans were demanding their $1000 army bonuses right away, claiming that they probably wouldn't live through the next war, so they wanted to enjoy their bonuses *before* going into battle.

The students also set up a group of Future Gold Star Mothers who wanted the Government to give them money for trips to Europe so they could visit the gravesites of their future sons and husbands.

Many adults thought the students' cynicism was horrible, reflecting the moral and patriotic decline of the younger generation. But pacifists were delighted with their young allies. As one religious pacifist journal noted in 1936, "To find among such students the complete disillusionment with respect to war, and the patriotism of former soldiers, is the best protection against future resort to arms."

There were many outstanding pacifist spokesmen during this era, and several of the most famous came from one organization—the Fellowship of Reconciliation (FOR). This was a radical Christian peace group whose members leaned toward absolute pacifism. Many of them were or had been Protestant ministers, and they were as concerned with social and economic evils as with pacifism.

FOR wanted to revamp society altogether, do away with the capitalist system, and close the gap between rich and poor. They felt that injustice and inequality were at the root of all violence, and that war would not end until all men were really equal. Many of the members were socialists of one type or another, who felt that the financial hardships and unrest of the 1930s were bound to happen under capitalism.

In believing that the social structure had to be changed in order to wipe out violence, FOR reflected some of Tolstoy's ideas. However, its members were not "nonresistants" like Tolstoy or like William Lloyd Garrison before him, who would use no weapon but love. They *would* resist evil, they said—but nonviolently. Thus, they could be called "nonviolent resisters."

Their inspiration came from the remarkable Indian leader Mohandas K. Gandhi, who was trying to throw off the yoke of British colonialism in India by means of a nonviolent revolution. Gandhi himself had been influenced by Tolstoy's ideas on nonviolence. But he took nonviolence several steps further, fusing it with Henry David Thoreau's ideas on civil disobedience as well as the ancient teachings of Hinduism. What Gandhi finally wound up with was his own unique philosophy for nonviolent action to force social change.

This was the first time that anyone had actually developed effective *techniques* for nonviolent resistance (also called passive resistance). Many times Gandhi and his followers simply refused to cooperate with their British rulers. Indian civil servants resigned their jobs; they renounced official titles and honors; they boycotted educational and cultural institutions. In the economic sphere they conducted strikes, sit-ins, marches, and boycotts. They weren't breaking any laws this way; they were just practicing noncooperation.

But the technique they used most often was civil disobedience. This did involve breaking laws, and suffering the penalties. The Indian resisters refused to pay their taxes or serve in the Army. Sometimes they manufactured products illegally, as a protest—such as when they openly made salt as part of their drive to end the state's salt monopoly.

Gandhi's famous Salt March to the sea was the climax of this nonviolent campaign. In addition, his followers launched a series of peaceful raids on the government salt depot. Without weapons or arms of any kind, the Indians tried to walk past the police who were guarding the depot. The police beat them, kicked them, and herded them off to jail, but the Indians never lifted a hand in violence. Gandhi kept up the pressure, and eventually the British were forced to negotiate the salt issue.

Over in America, FOR pacifists watched Gandhi's campaign with admiration. They were seeking a nonviolent alternative to class warfare, but they hadn't even gotten past the talking stage yet.

In only one instance did FOR members actually try Gandhi's tactics. During a 1936 strike of the Full Fashioned Hosiery Workers, several FOR members who belonged to the union organized a "lie-down" to prevent strikebreakers from entering the factory. Workers also stretched out in the middle of the road so that trucks on the way to the factory could not pass. However, in the end the police carted all the workers off to jail, and the strike failed.

As the threat of war loomed larger, FOR and other radical pacifist groups grew increasingly isolationist. Unlike the conservative peace groups, who began to favor alliances with the democratic countries of Europe, the radicals didn't want to do anything that might add to the risk of war. Many other Americans felt this way too, for the membership of the radical peace groups suddenly swelled. Between 1935 and 1941, the membership of FOR jumped from 4271 to 12,426. The War Resisters' League, a nonreligious radical peace group, also experienced rapid growth at this time.

Among the most famous spokesmen for the radical pacifists were the Reverend John Haynes Holmes, A. J. Muste, and Norman Thomas, all of whom belonged to FOR. As with so many other pacifists, their interests were far-flung, and they were caught up in many social causes —civil rights, civil liberties, socialism, the labor movement, and civic reform, to name just a few.

For each of them, pacifism was a religious belief. John Haynes Holmes was a product of the Harvard Divinity School, and he later became a Unitarian minister in the wealthy and conservative Church of the Messiah in New York.

But he was too restless, too intent on reforming the world to remain a conventional minister for very long. He became a Socialist and then a pacifist, holding firm to both beliefs during the oppressive days of World War I.

In 1919, he resigned from the Unitarian ministry, and established an independent church. He called it Community Church, and it was open to everyone—Catholics, Jews, Protestants, Hindus, Buddhists, and even atheists if they wanted to join. The members were not united by theology but by "democratic social idealism."

In addition to his other activities, Holmes edited a pacifist religious journal, *Unity,* and even tried his hand at writing for the theater. In 1936 he coauthored a play called *If This Be Treason,* which showed the power of pacifism in political affairs. He also wrote books on the relationship of religion to social problems.

Holmes was concerned with all men and with all forms of oppression. Although he was absolutely committed to peace, this didn't mean that he could just look aside while the fascists climbed to power in Europe. He showed his concern as early as 1933, when most Americans were not yet fully aware of the Nazi menace.

At that time, Rabbi Stephen Wise had arranged the first large-scale protest against Hitler in the United States. He had planned a massive march down Broadway, with thousands of Jews walking in grim silence. The protest was supposed to be an all-Jewish affair, since Rabbi Wise didn't think many other Americans were particularly interested. To his surprise, he was joined at the head of the procession by the Protestant minister John Haynes Holmes, the only Christian present among thousands of Jews.

Later on, both Holmes and Norman Thomas urged the United States to give asylum to Hitler's Jewish victims, but the polls showed that less than 8 percent of the American people cared to do this. In another survey, in 1939, Americans were asked if the United States should admit 10,000 refugee children from Germany, most of them Jewish. Sixty-one percent of Americans said no.

When learning of this, Norman Thomas remarked

acidly that most Americans seemed to want others to fight for the rights of Jews in Europe, rather than giving them asylum in America. Thomas and Holmes, on the other hand, preferred not to fight at all, but to save Hitler's victims by peaceful means.

Like Holmes, Norman Thomas also had a religious background. His father and grandfather were Protestant ministers, and he meant to follow in their footsteps. After graduating from Princeton, he trained for the ministry at Union Theological Seminary. Here he came under the influence of Dr. Walter Rauschenbusch and the Social Gospel—a doctrine that emphasized the church's role in social reform.

For the next few years, Thomas lived and worked as a minister among the Italian immigrants in East Harlem. The poverty, filth, and misery he saw there made him feel that the capitalist system was terribly unjust. In his autobiography he said that the actual experience of living with the poor, and enduring what they had to endure, drove him steadily toward socialism.

In 1916, Thomas joined the Fellowship of Reconciliation, which at that time was a very small Christian pacifist group. Soon he resigned his church post to work full time for FOR and to edit its monthly magazine, *The World Tomorrow*. He also became a member of the American Union Against Militarism, and in 1918 he took the big step of joining the Socialist Party—right in the middle of the war when the Socialists were at their peak of unpopularity.

He went on to head the Socialist Party, running for President of the United States on the Socialist ticket six times. Although he was known as "Mr. Socialist," many people thought of him as more of a social re-

former than a doctrinaire Marxist. The Communist Leon
Trotsky once derided him by saying, "Norman Thomas
called himself a Socialist as a result of a misunderstand-
ing."

Even though Thomas was a celebrated spokesman for
the working classes, they never really seemed to feel
that he was one of them. With his high-domed head,
narrow nose, and fine gray hair, he looked like a cul-
tured aristocrat. He often sounded like one, too, for he
used perfect English and came across as far more of an
intellectual than a "down-to-earth" labor man. However,
he was a superb public speaker who could electrify an
audience with every word and gesture.

In 1937, Thomas astounded many of his friends by
abandoning his pacifism temporarily during the Spanish
Civil War. Under the leadership of General Francisco
Franco, the Spanish fascists had attacked the moderate
left-wing government there, setting off bloody and bitter turmoil. Many of the European powers jumped into
the fray, with Germany and Italy helping the fascists
and Russia helping the loyalists.

Thomas and the New York Socialists got in touch
with the loyalists and agreed to organize a volunteer
battalion of well-trained young Americans to fight in
Spain. They intended to call it the Eugene Debs Column.
Thomas was willing to do this because he felt then that
fascism was an even greater evil than war—and because
he saw this as a battle between the working classes
and their oppressors. He didn't want the United States
to enter the conflict, but he did want to give whatever
support he could to the loyalists.

Thomas' action aroused a storm of protest among Socialists as well as pacifists, for most of them couldn't

condone violent class struggles. John Haynes Holmes lashed out against the "raising of an armed brigade and sending it to the battlefront to fight and kill." He also said that "to use the name of Gene Debs for this bloody business fills me with a horror which is indescribable."

A number of Socialists left the Party over this issue, and in Syracuse, New York, an entire chapter resigned. In the end, the Debs Column was never organized.

In supporting the Spanish loyalists, Thomas found himself working alongside many communists, who also supported them. But Thomas had always been fiercely anticommunist, and had led the fight to drive communists out of FOR and off the Board of Directors of the American Civil Liberties Union. The communists' demand for violent revolution appalled him, and he was afraid they might thwart the peaceful efforts of the other groups.

Thomas was never even tempted by communism, unlike his fellow pacifist and old friend A. J. Muste. Muste first met Thomas when both were students at the Union Theological Seminary. Muste also joined FOR in 1916, and went on to become its national chairman in 1926.

But within a few years, Muste had gotten deeply involved with revolutionary labor action. He left FOR, renounced his pacifism, and became a Trotskyite.

By 1936, however, he had another change of heart. At the annual conference of FOR he stood up before all his old friends and told them that he had come full circle— he believed in pacifism once again, with all the ardor of the repentant sinner. They responded by electing him to FOR's national council.

From that point on, Muste remained committed to

nonviolent social change. Perhaps more than any of his fellow pacifists, he was attracted to Gandhi's techniques and looked for ways to use nonviolent resistance in the struggle for the rights of labor.

Muste was more of a simple, plain-spoken man than Thomas. He was not given to dramatic oratory, and he seldom showed very much passion in his public speeches. At committee meetings he was often the last to speak up, for he liked to do a lot of listening. This was a rare quality among radicals, and as one friend said, "He's the only reformer I know who doesn't threaten other people's egos." In fact, Muste could sit still and listen to someone else talk for as long as two hours without ever once interrupting.

Muste had the typical idealist's impatience with money matters, and he didn't care very much about the material comforts of life. He got along without any bank account, earned only a small income from FOR, and never asked for a raise. A few times he actually refused raises, even though it often appeared that he had only one suit of clothes to his name.

One veteran of the labor battles recalled his first impression of Muste:

I was down and out, on strike, and my shoes were so thin I could feel the cold through the soles. All the do-gooders were on the platform to pep us up and raise the relief fund. I was in the first row of the audience, and right up above me, on the platform, was this long skinny fellow. I never saw such long legs on a man, and he kept crossing them to get them out of the way, but pretty soon they'd start swinging, and I saw the bottom of each of his shoes; the soles were gone and he had newspapers in them. I turned to the fellow next to me and asked him who it was. He said, "It's Muste. Used to be a preacher before he went straight."

Muste had a great influence in the labor movement. He used to lecture all over the country, spreading his ideas about nonviolent resistance and Gandhiism to all who would listen. He devoted his entire life to his pacifist ideals, for he was a leader in the cause from World War I days through the 1950s (with a few years out for his foray into communism).

One day in 1950, Muste talked to the students at Crozer Theological Seminary in Pennsylvania. Seated in the audience was a young man who listened avidly to Muste's speech, and came away deeply moved by the idea of achieving a social revolution through nonviolent resistance. The young man's name was Martin Luther King, Jr.

But this was in the future. In the 1930s, the United States was facing a different sort of upheaval. Germany had invaded first Czechoslovakia and then Poland, setting the stage for World War II.

From this point on, the pacifist movement in America declined. One by one, the conservative pacifists came to feel that Hitler's armies had to be stopped for the sake of humanity, and that war was a lesser evil than Nazism.

However, the more radical pacifists clung to their beliefs to the very end, still convinced that war wouldn't settle anything. Norman Thomas—who had returned to the pacifist fold after the Spanish Civil War—helped organize the Keep America Out of War Congress. To the dismay of many of his followers, he also spoke at meetings of the America First Committee, a right-wing isolationist group whose leading members were the aviator-hero Charles A. Lindbergh and Senator Robert A. Taft.

The America First Committee was suspected of being anti-Semitic and somewhat sympathetic toward Germany. But because it opposed war, Norman Thomas and some other pacifists cooperated with it in a very uncomfortable alliance. Oswald Garrison Villard was on its national board of directors when it was first organized, although he resigned within a month. Norman Thomas never joined the group, but many people thought he had because he spoke at their meetings, sharing the platform with Charles Lindbergh on one occasion.

Shortly after their joint appearance, Lindbergh delivered a very anti-Jewish speech in Des Moines, Iowa. He charged that the British, the Jews, and Roosevelt had formed an alliance to force the United States into the war. When Thomas heard of this, he publicly denounced Lindbergh as "a great idiot." But it was too late; the damage had already been done. Thomas' reputation was badly tarnished by his association with Lindbergh.

Many of Thomas' Socialist followers were very upset by his staunch isolationism. Unlike their antiwar stand during World War I, they wanted to oppose Germany now. Large numbers of them left the Party even before the Japanese attacked Pearl Harbor, and by January 1942, the Socialist Party had only 1141 members.

Socialists, and also many pacifists, had come to share editor William Allen White's feelings, which he expressed in a letter to his friend Oswald Garrison Villard in May 1941:

I hoped I would never see another war. I shall never encourage the coming of another war. But if it comes, this summer or next summer . . . I see nothing to do but to fight it with all our might and all our hearts. And that's not a pleasant prospect for a man who realizes the utter futility of wars in the past and who can only hope rather vainly that, out of this war, men may learn wisdom in the end.

Nazism had shattered the hopes of American pacifists. They viewed World War II with a sense of quiet despair, but since they had no alternatives to offer in the face of Hitler's barbarism, they felt it made no sense to mount an antiwar campaign. Their pacifism at this time was mainly a personal faith, evidenced mostly by their refusal to serve in the armed forces.

More than 6000 conscientious objectors spent the war years in jail because they did not meet the narrow religious requirements that would have entitled them to draft exemptions. This was far more than the total number of pacifists who went to jail during World War I, probably because pacifism was a more widespread philosophy by now. Many people had come to understand it better after the disillusionment following World War I, and the nation was not nearly as hostile to pacifists as it had once been. In almost every way (except in its treatment of Japanese-Americans), America was a far more tolerant country during World War II, and even the jailed war resisters were treated more kindly.

As a movement, however, pacifism was all but dead during the war years, at least as far as international affairs were concerned. But on the domestic scene, the philosophy of nonviolence was just beginning to come into its own.

9 "We Shall Overcome"

ONE EVENING IN JUNE 1943, a group of sixty-five blacks and whites got together in Chicago's Loop section. Their plan of action had been worked out ahead of time, and now they were about to carry it through.

First they split up into small parties of four and five, some all white, others mixed. Then, gradually, the various groups trickled into Stoner's Restaurant, a very posh and famous spot that had never admitted blacks before.

The all-white groups that entered the restaurant were seated immediately, but when the first interracial party arrived, the waiters ignored them. They stood in the front of the restaurant, waiting patiently and quietly, and paying no attention to the angry grumblings of the owner, Mr. Stoner. After an uncomfortable half hour, he decided it would be better to seat them, although he couldn't resist kicking one of the black men in the shins for revenge.

Within a few minutes, another interracial group entered. This time Stoner absolutely refused to seat them, and called the police. Quite unexpectedly, the police declined to arrest the group, since they were behaving in such a quiet and peaceful way. Stoner called the police three times, until finally they got so annoyed with him that they threatened to lock him up.

Meanwhile, business in the restaurant had come to a halt. About two hundred customers watched in silence while the interracial group remained standing. Other mixed groups had also entered by this time, and they were making plans to stay the night if they were not seated.

All of a sudden, an elderly white woman who was not connected with the demonstrators got up and invited a black girl to join her at her table. Taking a cue from this, the white demonstrators who had been seated earlier also invited the blacks to share their tables, until finally only two black men were left standing. At this point, the hostess in the restaurant came over to them and escorted them to a table.

Wild cheers rang out through the restaurant, and even the other patrons joined in the hurrahs. Nonviolent resistance had won out in this opening battle for civil rights.

The demonstration had been put on by a new pacifist civil rights group, the Congress of Racial Equality (CORE). This was an offshoot of the Fellowship of Reconciliation, and many of its leaders were also high-ranking members of FOR.

The idea for CORE was first put forward by James Farmer, a black pacifist who was race-relations secretary of FOR. Farmer wanted to set up a new group that would use Gandhian methods of nonviolent action to wipe out discrimination in America. He was backed by A. J. Muste, head of FOR, who had long advocated nonviolent resistance to force social change. In 1942, the first branch of CORE was set up in Chicago for the purpose of fomenting and planning a peaceful black revolution.

The founding of CORE marked a new stage in the evolution of radical pacifist thought in America. Beginning with William Lloyd Garrison in the 1840s, radical pacifists had regarded nonviolence as a total way of life. They applied it to domestic and personal affairs as well as international ones. In their view, slavery was evil because it rested on the forceful capture and suppression of one man by another. As they saw it, even governments did not have the right to use coercive force against lawbreakers. These pacifists would have done away with such instruments of force as policemen, soldiers, and jails, and relied only on the power of love and God.

This type of thinking was further explored by Tolstoy and his followers, who also had ultimate faith in the power of love. Many of these radical pacifists came to feel that the violence in the world sprang from unjust social and economic conditions, so that their pacifism became bound up with the quest for humanitarian reforms.

Gandhi took this philosophy a step further, turning nonviolence into a *method*—in his case, a method for forcing the British to end colonial rule in India. With him, nonviolence was not just a passive philosophy of love; it was a positive, dynamic technique for forcing social change, primarily through civil disobedience.

Gandhi's ideas filtered back to the United States, where a handful of black leaders seized upon them as a way of achieving racial equality without bloodshed.

Thus, radical pacifism—an idea that had started in the United States a century earlier, bloomed briefly in Russia, and then achieved dramatic success in India—was drifting back to the United States once again to usher in a new social revolution.

This type of pacifism had always been very different, and more religious in nature, than the conservative variety. The latter was geared mainly toward wiping out international warfare. Although the two groups often overlapped, conservative pacifists focused mainly on such goals as international arbitration and world congresses rather than domestic reform. They labored to make the League of Nations succeed; when it didn't, they began all over again, fastening their hopes on the United Nations.

In the years following World War II, conservative pacifists threw themselves into the battle to outlaw atomic weapons, ban nuclear testing, and get all nations to disarm. During the height of the Cold War, they formed such groups as the National Committee for a Sane Nuclear Policy (SANE), which was promptly accused by hardliners of being "soft on communism." (To most Americans at this time, "conservative" pacifists seemed very radical indeed. They were called "conservative" only in pacifist circles, but in the world at large they were thought of as liberals or left-wingers.)

While conservative pacifists concentrated on preventing nuclear war, radical pacifists were planting the seeds of a nonviolent black revolution in the United States.

Their successful integration of Stoner's Restaurant in Chicago was the first of many such nonviolent demonstrations. However, these methods did not draw widespread support from blacks right away—in fact, it took another seventeen years before the idea of sit-ins really caught on. In 1943, most blacks thought such tactics were far too militant, and feared that they would only arouse the anger of the white majority.

But CORE kept on. During the early years, its leaders were members of FOR, and its main offices were in FOR headquarters. A. J. Muste served as CORE's chief fund raiser for the first four years of its existence, and it was he who first encouraged young black pacifists to use radical nonviolent tactics. As Muste explained it:

I was not impressed with the sentimental, easygoing pacifism of the earlier part of the century. People then felt that if they sat and talked pleasantly of peace and love, they would solve the problems of the world. . . . nonviolence is not a negative thing. It does not mean the absence of violence, the renunciation of action, submission. It means resort to a superior form of struggle, the tapping of the reservoirs of moral force —"soul force" as Gandhi called it.

This type of passive resistance would unsettle an attacker, Muste felt. He wouldn't know how to cope with it, and he would lose his poise and self-confidence. In short, the attacker would be thrown off balance by a form of "moral jujitsu."

Among the men who shared Muste's views were James Farmer, a onetime theology student and the main organizer of CORE; Bayard Rustin, a black Quaker and ex-Communist; and George Houser, a white student at Union Theological Seminary who had gone to prison for refusing to register for the draft.

All of these pacifists yearned to bring about social justice, and they believed deeply in what Gandhi had told Afro-Americans: "With right, which is on their side," the Indian leader had said, "and nonviolence as their only weapon, if they will make it such, a bright future is assured."

In 1947, CORE launched the first "freedom ride" into the Deep South—only at that time it was called a "Journey of Reconciliation." Led by George Houser and Bayard Rustin, both of whom were secretaries in FOR, the "Journey" was a bold challenge to a long-standing southern custom.

The southern states were still enforcing "Jim Crow" seating arrangements even after a 1946 Supreme Court ruling had banned segregation in interstate travel. The Court's decision was simply ignored, until an interracial CORE team of sixteen men decided to test it by riding together through the South.

To their surprise, the riders were seldom abused by angry southern mobs. They were attacked just once, in Chapel Hill, North Carolina. However, the local police arrested them on six different occasions, so that the riders spent a good deal of time in jail.

Bayard Rustin was sentenced to work on a southern road gang, after which he wrote a pamphlet called *Twenty-Two Days on the Chain Gang at Roxboro, N.C.* This pamphlet touched off an investigation and shake-up of the brutal prison system there.

A bold and shrewd organizer, Bayard Rustin brought all the daring qualities of a guerrilla fighter to the non-violent civil rights campaign. He was a fiery speaker who could demolish an opponent on stage, and he was also a brilliant tactician.

He joined FOR after several conversations with A. J. Muste, and during the years they worked together they became very close. In Rustin's opinion, "Muste never made the mistake that many other pacifists have made. He didn't believe that lobbying and writing letters can be effective just by themselves. You have to act, and act with your body, in nonviolent demonstrations to create social dislocation."

Together with James Farmer and George Houser, Rustin led many lunch-counter sit-ins during the 1940s. These direct-action campaigns didn't receive much attention in the white press, but they did get some results. In Washington, D.C., these sit-ins resulted in the integration of many downtown establishments that were once closed to blacks. Included among them was the YMCA, whose manager finally relented after calling the black demands "trivial."

During the summers of 1947 and 1948, CORE mounted a full-scale campaign to desegregate the swimming pool at Palisades Amusement Park in New Jersey. Demonstrators formed long lines and refused to leave when denied admission. The park's owner told them, "You'll all be dead before I change"—a threat that very nearly came true. Several times the black demonstrators were severely beaten by thugs, winding up in the hospital with bloody heads, broken jaws, and busted ribs. Many of them were arrested by the police, often on trumped-up charges.

Because of all the violence, this was one campaign that the white press did pay attention to. Newspapers played up the incidents and condemned the segregation policy at Palisades. All the hullabaloo resulted in the passage of New Jersey's 1949 Civil Rights Act, which erased the color barrier at the amusement park and elsewhere.

Despite these early successes, CORE lost momentum over the next few years. It failed to attract a wide base of support among blacks, most of whom preferred the more proper and strictly legal tactics of the National Association for the Advancement of Colored People (NAACP). By the mid-1950s, CORE had only a few chapters and an income of less than $10,000 a year. It seemed as if the nonviolent revolution was dying a quiet death.

Then, in 1955, an historic event reawakened the direct-action movement and gave it one crucial element it had lacked before—an electrifying leader who could inspire and unite the black masses.

It started on December 1, 1955, in Montgomery, Alabama. Mrs. Rosa Parks, a black seamstress, was returning home after her day's work in a department store. Like most blacks in Montgomery, she traveled by bus. In fact, 70 percent of the daily bus riders in the city were black; they didn't own cars, whereas the majority of whites did.

Nevertheless, blacks were treated very shabbily by the Montgomery bus companies. They couldn't enter by the front door of the bus, although whites could. They couldn't sit in the front section, which was reserved exclusively for whites. Even if there were no whites on the bus at all, blacks were forced to stand rather than sit in the whites-only section. Furthermore, if the whites overflowed their own section, blacks had to get up and move further to the rear, giving up their seats to the whites. The rule was that no black could sit while a white stood.

When Mrs. Parks got on the bus that afternoon, it was fairly empty. She took a seat directly behind the whites-only section, and relaxed after her long, exhausting day's work. But soon the bus got crowded. A number of whites piled on until there were no more seats for them. The bus driver ordered Mrs. Parks and several other blacks to get up and move to the rear, where they would have to stand.

The other blacks did as they were told, but Mrs. Parks refused. Her feet hurt and she was tired, and the humiliation was suddenly more than she could bear. She had been humiliated every day of her life, and she just had enough—she wasn't about to give up her seat for anyone!

The bus driver called the police, who took her off the bus, brought her down to the station house, and booked her for violating Montgomery's segregation code. Trial was set for the following week.

Meanwhile, Mrs. Parks was free on bail, which had been provided by E. D. Nixon (no relation to Richard), who had been chairman of the Alabama NAACP and was a leading member of a militant labor union, the Brotherhood of Sleeping Car Porters.

Like many other blacks in Montgomery, Mr. Nixon was very upset over the constant humiliations meted out by the bus companies. These companies were thriving because of all the blacks who rode the buses; if they had to depend on white passengers, they'd be out of business before very long. Yet in recent months there had been a series of outrageous insults to black riders, the latest of which involved Mrs. Parks.

That night, Mr. Nixon couldn't sleep. The bus problem kept revolving in his mind, until finally he turned to his wife and said, "You know, I think every black person in town should stay off the buses for one day in protest for Mrs. Parks's arrest. What do you think?"

"I think you ought to stop daydreaming," she said. "Turn out that light and get some sleep."

The next morning, Mr. Nixon telephoned several black leaders in Montgomery to see what they thought of the idea. Among those he spoke to were Ralph Abernathy, pastor of the First Baptist Church, and Martin Luther King, Jr., who had just come to Montgomery the previous year as pastor of the Dexter Avenue Baptist Church.

They leaped at the idea of a bus boycott, and the news spread through the black community like a flash fire. The pastors of all the black churches announced the boycott from their pulpits; the black taxi companies agreed to transport people to and from work for ten cents; and thousands of leaflets were passed out in black neighborhoods.

Mrs. Parks had been arrested on Thursday, December 1. The following Monday, the city's buses were empty. Blacks walked to work, or rode together in car pools, or used the black taxi services. But they would not use the buses.

That day, the black leaders of Montgomery met to form a new organization that would lead the bus protest. They named it the Montgomery Improvement Association, and chose Martin Luther King, Jr., as its president.

In the evening, King spoke to the black people of Montgomery, who had poured into the Holt Street Church to hear their new leader. There wasn't nearly enough room for everyone, and more than 4000 blacks were massed outside. In this highly charged atmosphere, King took the pulpit to speak of the black people's hopes and dreams, and to outline the methods of their new movement.

First of all, he said, it would be peaceful. "In our protest there will be no cross burnings," King intoned in his rolling baritone voice. "No white person will be taken from his home by a hooded Negro mob and brutally murdered. There will be no threats and intimidations. We will be guided by the highest principles of law and order . . . Our method will be that of persuasion, not coercion. We will only say to the people 'Let your conscience be your guide.' Our actions must be guided by the deepest principles of our Christian faith. Love must be our regulating ideal . . .

"If you will protest courageously and yet with dignity and Christian love, when the history books are written in future generations, the historians will have to pause and say, 'There lived a great people—a black people—who injected new meaning and dignity into the veins of civilization.' This is our challenge and our overwhelming responsibility!"

The black people of Montgomery roared their approval. They voted to continue their boycott until they were guaranteed courteous treatment, fair and flexible seating arrangements, and the hiring of black drivers for routes in mainly black neighborhoods. The demands were certainly modest, but the white power structure would not yield. White leaders never had to negotiate with the black community before, and they didn't intend to start now.

The Montgomery bus boycott captured the attention of the entire nation. It went on for about a year, with 95 percent of the city's 50,000 black people refusing to ride the buses. Such unity, pride, and determination among thousands of blacks had never been seen before in a southern city. It was the beginning of the black revolution in America, and the first time that nonviolent resistance emerged as a mass movement.

As King said of the protest, "Christ furnished the spirit and motivation, while Gandhi furnished the method."

Throughout the year-long protest, all eyes were on Martin Luther King, Jr. He was the voice and the soul of the movement, and he gave it direction. But if he insisted on nonviolence among his people, his opponents did not. Day after day, King's life was threatened. He received abusive and obscene phone calls and letters, which began to shake him up after a while. His nerves grew taut; he was afraid. At times he thought of backing out, but he couldn't bring himself to do that either.

Finally he faced his fear head on. Speaking before a large crowd, he said: "If one day you find me sprawled out dead, I do not want you to retaliate with a single act of violence. I urge you to continue protesting with the same dignity and discipline you have shown so far."

In January 1956, King's house was bombed. He was not there at the time, but his wife and daughter were. Although they escaped unharmed, there was a great deal of damage to the house.

The incident threw the black community into a rage. As soon as word got around, thousands of blacks began massing outside King's home, armed with guns, knives, clubs, bottles, and rocks. Police and firemen were there too, facing the menacing mob in tense silence.

Just when a shoot-out seemed inevitable, King made his way onto the porch of his bombed-out home. "Don't get panicky!" he roared. "If you have weapons, take them home; if you do not have them, please do not seek to get them. We cannot solve this problem through retaliatory violence . . . We must love our white brothers no matter what they do to us. We must make them know that we love them. Jesus still cries out in words that echo across the centuries: 'Love your enemies; bless them that curse you; pray for them that despitefully use you.' This is what we must live by. We must meet hate with love.

"I did not start this boycott. I was asked by you to serve as your spokesman. I want it to be known the length and breadth of the land that if I am stopped this movement will not stop. What we are doing is just, and God is with us."

King's effect on the crowd was so strong that there was no violence at all. The people returned to their homes, having weathered the first major crisis of their movement. From then on, they remained steadfastly nonviolent.

Black leaders and pacifists from all over the country came to Montgomery to help out. Among the most welcome arrivals was Bayard Rustin, who had far more experience with nonviolent resistance than Martin Luther King. Rustin soon became King's secretary, and the two men worked closely together for many years.

The white leaders of Montgomery never gave in to the blacks' demands voluntarily, even though they were losing a great deal of money. The buses that normally brought crowds of black shoppers to the downtown stores remained empty—so the stores also lost business. But still the whites wouldn't give in. They were afraid that one black victory would lead to more, until the whites lost their dominance entirely. Finally, however, the decision was taken out of their hands.

In November 1956, the Supreme Court of the United States declared that Alabama's state and local laws requiring segregation on the buses were unconstitutional.

Shortly afterward, the black bus boycott in Montgomery came to an end. On December 21, Martin Luther King and a white coworker boarded a bus and sat down together—and no one stopped them. Officially, the era of Jim Crow was over, at least as far as the buses were concerned.

Unofficially, however, the battle still hadn't ended. In January 1957, four black churches and two black homes were dynamited. White snipers fired at buses, in one case hitting a black rider in the leg. Black passengers were beaten up from time to time, and someone blasted the front door of King's house with a shotgun.

But all of this was futile. The color line on the buses had been broken, and the Montgomery bus boycott went down in history as a stunning victory for blacks.

With the knowledge, strength and following that he had gained from this protest, Martin Luther King, Jr., went on to form the Southern Christian Leadership Conference, which called upon all blacks "to assert their human dignity" by rejecting "further cooperation with evil." Bayard Rustin helped King set up this organization, along with sixty other black leaders from ten southern states.

At this time, too, King joined FOR to further emphasize his deep faith in nonviolence. Although as a youth he had read Gandhi and had listened to A. J. Muste's speeches on nonviolent resistance, he had always been a little skeptical about the power of nonviolence.

Recalling his doubts, King said: "When I went to Montgomery, Alabama, as a pastor in 1954, I had not the slightest idea that I would later become involved in a crisis in which nonviolent resistance would be applicable . . . The experience in Montgomery did more to clarify my thinking on the question of nonviolence than all of the books that I had read. As the days unfolded, I became more and more convinced of the power of nonviolence. Living through the actual experience of the protest, nonviolence became more than a method to which I gave intellectual assent; it became a commitment to a way of life."

After the Montgomery bus boycott, King became a world-famous black leader. His successful protest sparked a new wave of black pride that flowed into all the civil rights groups. The NAACP reached its peak strength, making enormous strides in the law courts and scoring one landmark victory after another. CORE flourished as never before, with its membership and income more than doubling in the late 1950s. King's Southern Christian Leadership Conference gained an enormous following in the South, and blacks throughout the country looked to him for inspiration.

There were black marches to integrate the schools, protest meetings, speeches, and peaceful demonstrations. The pressure was on, and it seemed as if genuine racial equality was just around the corner.

But by 1960, it was becoming clear that the black victories were far greater on paper than in practice. Six years after the historic Supreme Court decision outlawing segregated schools, the vast majority of American schools were still segregated. So were many restaurants, theaters, parks, hotels, and other public places. Blacks still earned far less money than whites; they were still confined mainly to menial jobs; and they still lived under terrible slum conditions. Actually, despite all the agitation, very little had changed.

The black groups had been concentrating mainly on legal victories, but by now it seemed that this was not enough. King's organization had also applied other forms of noncooperation after the Montgomery boycott, but only CORE had actually tried civil disobedience. It still seemed too radical for a mass movement, but King and the other black leaders felt the time had come for an all-out nonviolent assault.

They had not yet planned their strategy when the movement suddenly caught fire spontaneously.

On February 1, 1960, four black freshmen from a college in Greensboro, North Carolina, walked into the local Woolworth Five-and-Ten and sat down at the lunch counter that was reserved for whites. No one would serve them, so they sat there from 10 A.M. until after midnight. They returned the next day, and the day after that.

On February 4, they were joined by black students from another college. News of their protest was beginning to spread, and within just a few days, black students had launched other lunch-counter sit-ins at Durham, Winston-Salem, and eight other North Carolina towns. Over the next two weeks, the student sit-ins spread to schools in South Carolina, Tennessee, and Virginia.

Workers from CORE, FOR, and the Southern Christian Leadership Conference raced to the scene to offer help and provide on-the-spot training in nonviolent resistance. The student movement had actually started without these older groups, even though they had been planting the seeds for years. Now, in their sudden haste to support the students, they recalled Gandhi's famous remark, "There go my people. I must hurry and catch up with them, for I am their leader."

The sit-ins spread rapidly throughout the South. In Orangeburg, South Carolina, CORE trained students for several days and then sent them out on a massive sit-in campaign that closed all the lunch counters in the downtown area. To cap the demonstration, 1000 students marched through the heart of town. Picket lines were thrown around all the Woolworth stores in Los Angeles and Boston, while eighty-six stores in New York were picketed. Two million leaflets were handed out, asking people to boycott the chain.

By the end of March, sit-ins, marches, and mass demonstrations were going on in fifty cities throughout the South to force an end to segregation. CORE held classes in nonviolent resistance, and for the most part the young demonstrators were peaceful. If they were called names, they kept quiet. If they were hit, they didn't strike back. If the police dragged them off to jail, sprayed them with tear gas or fire hoses, they didn't retaliate. Instead, they sang hymns—"We Shall Overcome" was a favorite—and said prayers. For inspiration they read Martin Luther King's *Stride Toward Freedom*, and Richard Gregg's *The Power of Non-Violence*.

To coordinate the activities of the students, the Southern Christian Leadership Conference helped set up a youth group—the Student Non-Violent Coordinating Committee (SNCC)—dedicated to the "philosophical or religious ideal of nonviolence."

King, Bayard Rustin, James Farmer, and Ralph Abernathy led hundreds of street demonstrations and sit-ins, and for a while the nonviolent revolution swept the country.

The sit-ins of 1960 were just the beginning of the civil-disobedience campaign. More than 3500 demonstrators were arrested in the first eight months of that year, but this was nothing compared to what lay ahead. The following year, in Birmingham, Alabama, more than 1000 demonstrators were arrested *in one day*, and the police unleashed their killer dogs on crowds of unarmed black men, women, and children. Such brutality touched off 758 black demonstrations in 186 cities over the next few weeks.

In 1963, there were 14,733 civil rights arrests. This was also the year of the historic "March on Washington," when Martin Luther King gave his impassioned speech to the cheering multitudes in front of the Lincoln Memorial, crying out, "I have a dream . . ." In 1964, King won the Nobel Peace Prize, crowning his leadership of the non-violent black revolution. He was now at the pinnacle of his power and influence.

His movement had inspired "Freedom Rides" into the Deep South, modeled after CORE's "Journey of Reconciliation" years before, as well as highly publicized, intensive voter-registration drives among the black masses. Scores of whites and blacks had paid for their idealism with their lives, and thousands more were injured during demonstrations.

But after a while, disillusionment set in. The non-violent movement had succeeded in its original goal—wiping out segregation (legal segregation, that is). But that didn't seem to be enough any more, particularly among the younger generation of blacks, who were demanding far more than their parents. They had grown up *expecting* equality, only to find that they, too, were second-class citizens. Housing patterns were still divided along racial lines, and so were most schools. Blacks were still poor compared to whites, and they still had very little say in the American power structure.

For years, blacks had thrown themselves bodily into the drive for equality. Now they were exhausted, and as far as they could see, they didn't have very much to show for their pains. They weren't even sure that their celebrated victories were worth very much.

As one angry student put it, "All those people died,

and for what? Just so we could sit next to Whitey at some broken-down lunch counter and eat an indigestible hamburger?"

By the mid-1960s, a change came over the civil rights movement. Younger, more militant blacks grew restive under the policy of nonviolence. They didn't believe in the power of love any more. They had begun to hate.

New leaders emerged, such as Stokely Carmichael, who first issued the clarion call for "Black Power." Whereas King and the older black leaders had worked alongside whites to integrate the country, Carmichael declared, "If we are to proceed toward liberation, we must cut ourselves off from white people. We must form our own institutions, credit unions, co-ops, political parties, and write our own histories."

The new spokesmen were far more militant than the old, and more inclined toward violence, if necessary. Under Carmichael's leadership, the Student Non-Violent Coordinating Committee stopped being a pacifist civil-rights group. Carmichael's successor, H. Rap Brown, led SNCC even further away from nonviolence, so that critics began calling it "the Non-Student Violent Coordinating Committee." Even CORE—a long-time pacifist group that had always been well-integrated—came out in favor of black power.

The mood of the militants grew increasingly antiwhite and angry, and whites started drifting away from the civil rights movement. Once they were no longer welcome in leadership roles, they began to lose interest altogether. The honeymoon between blacks and whites was over. Race riots broke out in the northern black ghettos—Harlem, Watts, Detroit, Newark, and Washington, D.C., were just a few of the places that were ravaged by fiery outbursts during the riot-torn summers of 1964–68.

Revolutionary groups like the Black Panthers began to attract the young, who showed a growing contempt for Martin Luther King's devotion to nonviolent protest.

Just as King was desperately searching for new ways to reawaken his people's faith in nonviolence, he was struck down by an assassin. The black apostle of nonviolence died violently—just as Gandhi had.

His movement had reached its peak in the first half of the 1960s, but even before his death it had begun to lose vigor. Now that he was gone, it was rapidly giving way to the more strident voices of the angry black revolutionaries, who talked of "guerrilla wars" and "liberation struggles."

Ironically, while the philosophy of nonviolence was losing ground on the home front, pacifists were gaining power on the international scene. In fact, the American people as a whole were turning away from the civil rights struggle and paying more attention to what was happening overseas.

10 Vietnam!

THERE WAS a war on.

Americans hadn't realized it at first, but their soldiers were dying in Vietnam. It was the kind of war that had snuck up on people rather quietly.

American military advisers had gone into Vietnam as far back as 1954, after France had given up all hope of maintaining her colonial grip on the area. When France pulled out, her Indochina empire was split up into several new, independent nations—Laos, Cambodia, South Vietnam, and communist North Vietnam. The United States, fearing that the communists would also take over South Vietnam after France's withdrawal, stepped into the breach with money and war supplies to help the feeble regime of President Ngo Dinh Diem.

All this took place at the height of the Cold War. At that time, American strategists saw South Vietnam as a pivotal spot—if it fell to the communists, all the other countries of southeast Asia might topple along with it, like a row of dominoes. This was the famous "domino theory" on which America's policy in Vietnam rested.

From 1954 to 1959, an uneasy peace existed in South

Vietnam. With American support, President Diem seemed to have the communists under control. But then, in 1959, the Viet Cong launched an offensive drive, gaining control of many villages and rural areas. President Diem hung on to the cities and some coastal areas, but his grip was very shaky.

In 1961, the American General Maxwell D. Taylor visited South Vietnam and drafted a top-secret report on conditions in the country. He said the situation was very grave, and urged President John F. Kennedy to send arms, men, helicopters, and money immediately. At the time, there were only about 800 American military advisers in Vietnam, and General Taylor felt this was not nearly enough.

To meet the emergency, the United States established a new American military organization in South Vietnam—the Military Assistance Command—under the leadership of General Paul D. Harkins. After that, American military personnel began swarming into the country.

By 1963, about 10,000 United States troops were "helping out" in Vietnam. Ostensibly, they were not there to fight, but to "advise and support" the Vietnamese. However, this was quite a sizable chunk of advisers for a small country to digest, and it wasn't long before newspapermen began reporting that they had seen American officers in battle and on combat missions. The United States Government kept denying that American soldiers were doing anything more than training the Vietnamese and fighting only when attacked, but it was getting harder to explain the growing list of American casualties.

Finally, in 1965, all pretense was over. President Lyndon B. Johnson ordered a massive military build-up in Vietnam, and hundreds of thousands of Americans were

sent there to fight. The United States was now wholly involved in an undeclared war.

Until this time, there had been only a smattering of
antiwar protest in the United States. Pacifist energy had
been channeled mainly into two other areas—the nonviolent civil rights movement and the campaign to outlaw
nuclear weapons.

Ever since the United States had first unleashed its
atomic bomb on Japan in 1945, the fear of an earth-shat-
tering nuclear holocaust hung heavily over the world.
The United States and the Soviet Union faced each
other menacingly across the chasm of the Cold War, and
at times it seemed as if a nuclear outburst would be
inevitable.

But with the signing of the nuclear test ban treaty by
the United States and Russia in 1963, and a general
thaw in Soviet-American relations, the danger of a nuclear holocaust declined. Pacifists felt they had made a
real breakthrough in this area, for it seemed much less
likely now that the human race would be wiped out by
hydrogen bombs.

These pacifists now began to look at what was happening in Vietnam—and before long they stopped worrying about H-bombs and started worrying about napalm.

At about the same time, white pacifists in the civil
rights movement began to feel that they were unwelcome
allies in the eyes of many blacks. With the new stress on
"black power" rather than integration, whites were eased
out of such organizations as CORE and SNCC. Also,
the movement itself was split, with the militant young
black revolutionaries questioning the nonviolent ap-
proach of Martin Luther King, the NAACP, and the
Urban League.

Because of this dissension, many white pacifists began drifting away from civil rights work and into the growing antiwar movement. When President Johnson escalated the war in 1965, the impact made pacifists join together in full strength, amassing the biggest antiwar campaign this country had ever seen.

In previous eras, pacifists had never been able to prevent wars, but wars usually snuffed out pacifist movements. As soon as the first shot was fired, pacifists tended to put aside their protests and support their country, or at least remain quiet. The most vocal opposition in the midst of war usually came from other sources—from the white working class during the Civil War, and from Socialists and Wobblies during World War I.

But the Vietnam War was different. Here, pacifist sentiment reached a feverish pitch *during* the war, not *before* it. What's more, the antiwar movement drew hundreds of thousands of nonpacifists as well—people who were not against *all* wars, only this *particular* one.

In short, what made the Vietnam War different from other wars was that so many Americans—pacifists and nonpacifists alike—were united in their belief that it was *unjust*.

The United States had intervened in what was basically a civil war in order to prop up a feeble anticommunist regime in South Vietnam. The fact that the regime was not democratic, and did not have much popular support from its own people, did not seem to matter much to American strategists. They felt that vital United States interests were at stake here.

But many Americans didn't share this view. Now that the chill was out of the Cold War, they had stopped believing that communism in southeast Asia was a dire threat to the United States. They saw that America was bombing Vietnamese villages, defoliating the forests with napalm, uprooting millions of people, slaughtering civilians, and wreaking destruction everywhere—just to save the Vietnamese people from the horrors of communism. To make matters worse, the Vietnamese themselves didn't seem to care if the communists took over or not; they only wanted to be left alone.

Between 1965 and 1968, American antiwar protests reached an ear-splitting crescendo. There were massive peace parades, marches on Washington, strikes for peace, and antiwar rallies from coast to coast. War protesters blocked troop trains, tried to close down draft boards, and interfered with the recruitment of soldiers.

President Johnson was unable to convince the American people of any real need for this war. Distrust and dislike of him grew so strong that he withdrew from the presidential race in 1968 rather than risk a humiliating defeat.

His successor, Richard Nixon, came into office on a promise to seek an "honorable" peace, but four years later American troops were still fighting in Vietnam. Although the number of American soldiers was much smaller than before, the war was still not over. Despite all the protests at home, President Nixon had not yet been able to find a face-saving way out.

The unpopularity of the Vietnam War posed some very grave problems—particularly for the boys who were being asked to risk their lives in it. Not many were eager to serve, and as the war dragged on, the number of conscientious objectors swelled enormously. There was constant pressure on the courts and the Government to expand the grounds for draft exemptions.

Under the old laws, only religious pacifists could qualify as conscientious objectors. During World War I, the draft law exempted only members of "well-recognized religious sects . . . whose . . . principles forbid its members to participate in war in any form."

In practice, this meant that almost the only ones who could qualify were Quakers or Mennonites. Other religious pacifist sects were not "well-recognized."

Jehovah's Witnesses were a special case by themselves. Although they were a large and well-known sect, their religion required them to fight in one war—the final, God-ordained battle of Armageddon. Thus, they couldn't qualify for draft exemptions because their religion didn't forbid war "in any form."

During World War II, the draft law was relaxed somewhat. Exemptions were granted to anyone who "by reason of religious training and belief is conscientiously opposed to participation in war in any form." Instead of going off to battle, these objectors could either perform noncombatant service or do civilian work of national importance.

But this still didn't leave any way out for men who were deeply opposed to war for moral or philosophical reasons, rather than religious ones. Also, it made no allowances for men who were against a *particular* war, but not all wars in general.

This was the main problem facing many draftees in the Vietnam War. They might have willingly gone off to fight in other battles, but they felt that this particular conflict was immoral. Even though the Supreme Court was now interpreting the draft law more broadly—saying that men could qualify as conscientious objectors for purely moral and ethical reasons—they still had to be against *all* wars. In March 1971, the Court had ruled that men were not entitled to conscientious objector status if they opposed only "unjust" wars.

This left many young men without any avenue of escape. They either had to fight, and possibly die, in a war they felt was wrong—or they had to pay the consequences of their refusal, namely jail.

Because of this dilemma, much of the antiwar movement took the form of draft resistance and draft obstruction. Draft-card-burning rallies were held in public parks, in full view of TV cameras and the police. Such prominent men as Dr. Benjamin Spock, the famous baby doctor, were arrested and tried for counseling young men on ways to evade the draft.

Two Catholic priests—Daniel and Philip Berrigan—first captured the nation's attention by raiding the draft office in Catonsville, Maryland, pouring napalm and blood on draft records, and then burning the documents. Seven other war resisters carried out this action along with the Berrigan brothers, and the group became known as the "Catonsville Nine."

Their dramatic protest touched off a whole series of draft-office raids by Catholic activists, including other priests and nuns. In August 1971, the FBI captured a group of twenty-five war opponents who were allegedly planning to raid Federal offices in Camden, New Jersey, and Buffalo, New York. Several Catholic priests and a Lutheran minister were among those arrested.

The emergence of the Catholic clergy in the peace movement was a totally new phenomenon. Most Catholics had not been attracted to pacifism before, largely

because the Catholic Church had always sanctioned
"just" wars—and the Church had the final say on which
wars were "just" and which were not. If a Catholic
opposed *all* wars, he would be going against his church.
For this reason, it was rare to find Catholic pacifists.

The main outlet for Catholic pacifism in the United
States had been the Catholic Worker movement, founded
by Dorothy Day in 1933. This group combined pacifism
with religious, radical, and anarchist beliefs. It published a newspaper, *The Catholic Worker,* with a cir-
culation of 110,000; ran Houses of Hospitality in thirty
cities to help the poor; and founded several farming
communes. But the Worker was a unique type of organization, and far too radical for most Catholics.

It wasn't until the Vietnam War that Catholics began
joining the peace groups in large numbers. Like many
other Americans, they were convinced that this war was
immoral and that they could oppose it in good conscience. Also, there was a revolution going on within
the Catholic Church itself, with many young, radical
priests rebelling against the religious dogma laid down
centuries ago.

Some of these radical priests wound up in the fore-
front of the antiwar movement, where they practiced
Gandhian techniques of nonviolent resistance. The Ber-
rigans' library contains all of Gandhi's writings, and both
brothers have dedicated themselves to nonviolence. It
may be argued that destroying government property is
not a nonviolent action, but many of today's radical
pacifists don't see it that way. They feel they are up
against an unyielding war machine, and must fight it as
best they can *without bloodshed.*

This sets them apart from revolutionary groups like

the Weathermen, who have blown up buildings and killed innocent people as part of their antiwar outrage. Daniel Berrigan has called this type of protest "the wildest kind of egotistical violence." But he, too, is pessimistic about America's future, noting that "the times are inexpressibly evil," and that there are no lawful remedies left.

"Let me say as plainly as I know how," he declared, "I don't see as a politic tactic that anything that might be called 'useful' is left to us, except civil disobedience. I say that openly . . . I don't see anything remaining to us by way of confronting the warmakers, except civil disobedience."

11 "Hell No! We Won't Go!"

ONE OF THE TRAGEDIES of the Vietnam War is that it has turned so many young Americans against their own country. They believe that America is waging an unjust fight, and they don't want to have anything to do with it.

Young men who might have been loyal, law-abiding citizens now find themselves rebels—even criminals—because their consciences won't let them participate in a war they feel is unjust.

In 1968, Dr. Willard Gaylin began a study of some nonreligious war resisters who had willingly gone to jail for their beliefs. He found that on the whole they were very high-minded, idealistic young men who were not trying to tear down their country but to uplift it. They came from all sorts of backgrounds. Some were total pacifists, some were not. But most of them shared a belief that their actions were helping to make America a better place.

Dr. Gaylin's project was extended over a two-year period and involved 26 non-religious objectors in two different prisons. Of these, 22 were white and 4 were black; 12 came from Catholic families and 14 from Protestant homes. None were Jewish—a surprising fact since a large percentage of *college* antiwar activists were Jewish, while only a small percentage were Catholic. Dr. Gaylin noted that this "immediately suggests that the imprisoned war resisters are a different population from the college radicals."

Dr. Gaylin delved deeply into the private lives and personalities of his subjects. Perhaps the most intellectual of the group was Matthew. (Dr. Gaylin used fictitious names to protect his subjects.) Far from being a breast-beating zealot, Matthew was a soft-spoken young man who sprinkled his talk with references to writers and philosophers. He wore large horn-rimmed glasses and puffed steadily on an unlit pipe. He seemed controlled and unemotional, although he could erupt in sudden anger. In short, he appeared to be the very model of a scholar, and looked oddly out of place in his sacklike prison denims.

Matthew did not have to be in jail. He was a Quaker by birth, and could easily have gotten a draft exemption on religious grounds. However, he felt it would have been unethical to claim a religious exemption when, in fact, he was not religious. In his extreme concern about his own morality, and about the effect his actions might have on others, he chose jail. It seemed more honest to him.

Matthew came from an upper-middle-class suburban home in which he was the oldest of five children. (Curiously, all but five of the war resisters in both prisons were eldest sons.) Matthew's father was a nuclear physicist who worked on government projects. He was away a lot of the time, but when he was home his imposing, towering personality dominated the household. Matthew respected and admired his father, but was also a little afraid of him.

The older man was a somewhat aloof, mysterious figure who was engaged in highly classified work. Yet he was also an offbeat character who rode a bicycle to his office every day and displayed copies of the *Worker* (the Communist Party newspaper) on his coffee table just to confuse the FBI agents who made periodic security checks on him.

As Matthew recalled: "We had a sort of ambiguous position in town. A great many of the people who lived in the community worked for my father, so everybody sort of deferred to us, and yet on the other hand we were thought of as sort of weird people.

"It was well-known in town that we were all atheists . . . We were thought of as slightly deviant. We didn't entertain as much as people thought we should, and when we had guests—like ladies for tea, which my mother hated doing but felt she had to—well, she would invite her maid to sit down to chat with them. This sort of scandalized the neighbors."

Matthew described his parents, and especially his father, as left-wing on social issues and right-wing on economic ones. The elder man was a Republican who loathed labor unions, but could become passionate on behalf of racial equality.

Coming from this type of individualistic family where social idealism flourished, Matthew drifted easily into the civil rights movement that sprang up in the early 1960s. While a student at Swarthmore College, he spent his summers in the Deep South working for the NAACP and other civil rights organizations. Here he came face to face with some of the more brutal realities of American life—he was thrown in jail several times, and was frequently pushed around and clubbed by southern officials who were doggedly determined to keep blacks "in their place."

At about this time, Matthew came to the conclusion that he had to dissociate himself from all sorts of organized brutality—including war. He felt that America had become preoccupied with "policing the world," and in November 1960, he sent his draft card back to Uncle Sam.

At the time Matthew took this step, the United States had not yet become heavily involved in Vietnam. American military advisers were stationed there, but American soldiers were not going on combat missions. The years of rapid escalation and eventual disillusionment were still to come, so that Matthew's antiwar stand was well ahead of its time. Matthew was among the earliest participants in the two major social uprisings of his era— the civil rights movement and the antiwar movement— and he was drawn to both because of his loathing of violence and oppression.

Another war resister—Hank—was very different from Matthew in most ways. Hank was a frail-looking black youth whose thick eyeglasses dominated his narrow, finely chiseled face. He had thought his poor eyesight would keep him out of the Army, but his draft board felt that as long as he could see the enemy, he could shoulder a rifle. Rather than go to Vietnam, he went to jail.

Hank's opposition to the war grew out of the black revolution that was taking place in the United States, rather than from any deep-rooted pacifist feelings. He could not see how America's military policy in Asia had any relevance for blacks back home, and did not want to fight in a war that meant nothing to him.

He was a gentle sort of person to begin with, and couldn't stand senseless violence. As he said, "I don't like to see blood for any reason. In fact, it's hard for me to work at the [prison] hospital because I don't like inflicting pain. It's hard for me to give someone an injection. Guys were all panning me about that last week."

However, as his prison term dragged on, he became more attracted to violence. He began a weight-lifting routine that added twenty pounds of muscle to his skinny frame because he wanted to "prepare" himself for when he got out. Although he used to reject the black liberation groups that advocated violence, he was now thinking about joining them. Prison life was changing a gentle young man into a violent one, and sometimes the change alarmed him.

He recalled the following incident: "Over in the mess hall the other day, I got up and took a tray to the table and this dude backed into me and I spilled my milk. I set it on the table, and he just stood there looking a little confused, and I said, 'You could say excuse me, you ——,' and I was just that close to going off at him. It not only shocked me, it shocked the people I was with. The violence, they hadn't seen me like that. I found myself getting tighter."

Like Matthew, Hank also had other alternatives than jail. He was a talented jazz musician, and had gotten a job offer in Sweden. But he felt he couldn't leave the country because that would be "copping out" on other blacks who were also resisting the draft. Most of them had no way out at all, and Hank felt he had a responsibility to stay and encourage them by his example.

Politically, Hank was still drifting. As a child, he had become familiar with poverty, hunger, and bigotry, all of which led him to join CORE during his junior year in high school. He worked in the voter-registration drive in Mississippi in 1965, and after that he became something of a Marxist. He joined several leftist political groups, including a Trotskyite organization, although he really wasn't quite sure what being a Trotskyite meant.

By the time he was of draft age, his politics had become a vague blend of socialism and black liberation, with strong emphasis on the latter. At his trial he had worn a bushy Afro hair style and a dashiki, even though he was sure it would make the judge less sympathetic to his case, and possibly even mean a longer sentence.

When Dr. Gaylin asked him if looking that way in court was worth a year or two of his life, he replied, "That's all of my life. Man, don't you know that's what it's all about? Am I free to have my style, am I free to have my hair, am I free to have my skin?"

Tim was another draft resister whose political direction was uncertain. The oldest of seven children, Tim was an open, warm-hearted and affectionate young man who could be very deeply moved by other people's troubles. His compassionate nature had led him into poverty work and the antiwar movement, but after spending some time in prison, his thoughts were confused; he was no longer sure that pacifism was his "bag."

Tim came from an unstable home, with parents who were always on the verge of splitting up but didn't because of their religion.

His mother was a librarian and his father was a traveling salesman who had a lot of trouble with liquor and gambling. Often he would blow his paycheck as soon as he got it, so that the family was constantly facing a money crisis. However, there were also times when he would buckle down and become a high-powered salesman, bringing home fat rolls of money. During one of these boom periods, the family bought a house in the suburbs. They also struggled to pay for expensive summer vacations and other luxuries.

When Tim got older and began sorting out values for himself, he took a vow of poverty and went to work helping the poor. He also became caught up in the peace movement.

"At one time," he said, "I thought to become a complete and total pacifist would be a fine way to develop yourself. I don't think so any more. As I go along I keep changing my motives for not being in the Army, but my conviction remains just as strong. I don't believe in this war and I don't believe in the domination of the weak by the strong. I have yet to develop a philosophy of which I'm convinced."

Shortly before going into prison, Tim had drifted into a hippie-like way of life. He found a small apartment in the rear of a vacant store, and even though people could look in from the street, he felt comfortable there. Since he never locked the door, neighborhood children wandered in and out. At first they thought he was peculiar, with his long, reddish-blond hair and his old baggy clothes, but soon they felt at ease with him. He worked part time to support himself, and was trying to become skilled as a sandalmaker when the draft caught up with him.

Tim never thought of himself as a hippie, although everyone else probably did. He regarded hippies as "hard-core drug people," while he was very much against drugs. The aspects of hippie culture that did appeal to him were communal living, the de-emphasis on physical and material needs, tolerance of others, and an emphasis on love.

The other war resisters that Dr. Gaylin studied were as different in personality, temperament, and background as the three already described. Bill was a slow-talking, solid New England farm boy who had been studying Greek and Latin at Harvard. He had grown up on a run-down turkey farm owned by his father, a hard-working man who read poetry in his spare time and occasionally wrote poems himself.

When Bill was in high school he became an absolute pacifist, opposed to all wars and violence of any sort. He was so dedicated to nonviolence that he would have let anyone beat him up anytime without even raising a hand in his own defense. But gradually his ardor faded, and by the time he reached draft age he no longer believed in total pacifism. He might have faked it to get an exemption, but this was against his principles. Also, he thought that if enough men went to jail rather than fight in Vietnam, it might create chaos in the draft system.

Bill's close friend and fellow prisoner Paul was the scion of a wealthy, old-line southern family. A pale, blond, well-mannered young man of twenty-one, Paul felt he was being more patriotic in going to jail than in fighting an unjust war. Patriotism meant a great deal to him—except his concept of patriotism was very different from the Government's.

Paul felt it was in the best interests of America to pull out of Vietnam immediately, and he simply would not fight in a self-defeating, ruinous war. Nor could he leave to avoid the draft. "It's my country, and I'm not going to run away from it," he said.

Paul's father, a retired diplomat and an authority on American history, felt that Paul had disgraced the family by his antiwar stand. The elder man was a very stern disciplinarian with a strong sense of social superiority and a belief in a strict class structure. Paul rejected these beliefs, but shared his father's deep feelings for the country.

However, prison life had a corrosive effect on these feelings. By the end of his first year in jail, he had already changed. As he remarked, "You know, I used to have such faith in the liberal tradition of law and justice. Perhaps it's just plain cynicism. The country, that nationalistic part, whatever it was that I attached myself to, just doesn't seem to be there any more. Not that when I get out I will do anything wrong or against the country. I'm sure I'll never break a law, except politically. But I don't think I'll ever be motivated again by what used to be a great respect and even love for the country, and that was the pillar of my existence."

John, who also came from a wealthy family, went to prep school and, finally, dropped out of Dartmouth to participate in the civil rights movement. For this act of defiance his father disowned him.

But John never wanted to lead the same kind of life as his father, who had struggled for success and achieved it—but never really enjoyed the money, social position, or prestige that went with it. He drank too much and had many bitter fights with John's mother, sometimes slapping her around a little.

In rejecting "phony" values, John threw his energies into the civil rights and antiwar movements. He felt that going to jail was the best way to combat the war and end the draft. He wouldn't leave the country because "I have always felt that one has to stay and fight for what one believes." Even as a prisoner he held on to his faith in America, saying, "If I ever get to the point where I feel hopeless about changing this country, then I might go some place else . . . Right now I still feel there is hope . . ."

This type of idealism—this belief that their actions might help make America a better place—was shared by most of the war resisters in Dr. Gaylin's study. They were high-minded, sensitive people who wanted to reform America, not destroy it, and they were willing to go to jail in order to live up to their own idea of what was right.

Although the majority had been absolute pacifists at one time or another, the feeling among them now was that this particular war was immoral. That was their main reason for refusing to fight. They were also very much aware that other young men across the nation might be inspired by their actions, so they felt they were serving a noble purpose in choosing jail.

Many of them could have avoided the Army without going to jail, such as the partially crippled youth who would certainly have flunked the Army's physical examination if he had taken it. But he refused. He *wanted* to be imprisoned as a war resister because this was the best way he could think of to show his intense antiwar feelings.

Dr. Gaylin found that prison affected these men in ways they hadn't foreseen. Most of them had been afraid of the physical side of prison life—the possibility of beatings or homosexual attacks. They hadn't realized the deadly effect that loss of freedom could have on their minds and spirits. Also, they were taunted and disdained by most of the other convicts, who seemed to feel that it was more acceptable to rob a bank than to insult flag or country.

Many of the war resisters were far less idealistic and less gentle when they left prison than when they had entered. Ironically, a number of them said they would now consider using violence—not against the Viet Cong, but against the American establishment that was waging the war. As one of them remarked, "The longer I'm here, the more doubt I have about the effectiveness of write-ins, literature, marches, or any of those things. Perhaps the only effective things in terms of the blacks, the poor whites, even the young—perhaps the only thing —is violence."

Another commented, "I had never been drawn to the more destructive kinds of social action. But now I'm feeling helpless. I don't know where to turn. Emotionally I'm ready to begin destroying, even though intellectually I feel protest must be creative or it's useless."

A third said, "I think we all made a serious mistake. I think our Government is too insensitive to respond to anything except violence and destruction."

These were the voices of men who were once deeply committed to the concept of nonviolence.

Only a tiny fraction of the young men who opposed the Vietnam War were idealistic enough or strong-minded enough to go to jail for their beliefs. Far greater numbers reluctantly obeyed their draft orders, while many others found ways to evade the Army without going to prison.

These draft evaders were not pacifists in the absolute sense, but men who were morally or politically opposed to the Vietnam War. Just like the men in jail, they couldn't qualify for exemptions as conscientious objectors because they weren't against all wars, nor were they motivated by religion. Most of them would probably not have questioned the need to go off and fight the Nazis in World War II, but the current war just didn't make any sense to them. What good was it doing? What was it all about? They felt they had not been given any good reason for risking their lives or for inflicting so much suffering on the Vietnamese people, and they were determined not to fight.

Many of them tried familiar dodges—faking homosexuality or mental illness; starving themselves so that they would weigh in under the acceptable minimum; popping pills or shooting dope to flunk the army physical; aggravating old injuries; getting falsified letters from medical doctors or psychiatrists. Other alternatives, before the lottery system was put into effect, were to go to school indefinitely or to take certain jobs that carried draft deferments, like industrial defense work or teaching.

Draft evaders who chose these methods were trying to get along within "the system." They may have disagreed with their country's policies and been unwilling to fight, but they still wanted to live a normal life, American style. They didn't want any part of prison.

Large numbers of them were very successful in staying out of the Army, particularly the educated youngsters from comfortable middle-class homes who knew where to go for draft counseling or other assistance. The poorer and less educated didn't have as many options open to them. In fact, in a lot of cases, they weren't even aware that other choices existed; when Uncle Sam called, they just went. The lottery system was intended to eliminate such injustices, but it didn't really touch the heart of the problem—the unpopularity of the Vietnam War.

For the more radical or the more disillusioned war resisters, there were still two other choices—to leave the country or to go "underground."

Whole colonies of young Americans in exile sprang up in Canada and the Scandinavian countries, the most popular havens for draft evaders. In 1970, Representative Edward Koch of New York took a firsthand look at the situation in Canada, and estimated that between 45,000 and 60,000 young Americans had fled there since 1965.

Canadians were sympathetic to these resisters, and the country did not extradite men for violating the U. S. Selective Service Act. But in order for an American to remain in Canada indefinitely, he had to be qualified as a "landed immigrant" by the Canadian Government. Whether or not a person could obtain this status rested on a combination of factors—schooling, vocational skills, age, the promise of a job in Canada, some knowledge of French, and such personal qualities as resourcefulness, motivation, and suitability to the culture of the country.

Americans who were lucky enough to qualify as "landed immigrants" were accepted as permanent residents, and could apply for Canadian citizenship in five years. Those who did not qualify faced the threat of deportation once their tourist visit limit expired—and if they were sent back to America, they would go to jail for draft dodging.

For many, the situation was very bleak. One young man who fled to Montreal gave the following picture of the exiles' existence there:

"I'm one of the lucky ones. In the first place, I arrived

with a substantial sum of money, and I got a job long before that ran out. Most of the evaders here, and even more so the deserters [from the U. S. Army], are desperately poor. They live in the hostels provided by the antiwar, antidraft aid groups here, or with some Canadian families who want to help, or two or three of them to a furnished room. Many of them have a lot of trouble finding work, especially if they don't have a college education or any skills. They hang around the hostels, or one another's rooms. There are whole blocks around here, and I understand in Vancouver and Toronto, too, where it's practically a solid community of American draft evaders and deserters. They have nothing to do, no money, no real place in the country around them, and they get very discouraged. A few of them finally give up and go back to the States."

Even for those Americans who manage to fit into Canadian life, it's still hard. The young man in Montreal said that several months after he got there "an immense depression settled over me. I don't mean right after I first arrived, when I was busy looking for an apartment, a job, and getting used to a strange city. I mean after that was all over and I settled down to work and live here. Only then it really struck me: My God, I'm an exile, I'm going to have to live outside my own country for the rest of my life."

Other draft evaders choose to remain in America but to live outside "the system." That is, they go underground, destroying all official records of themselves that people usually carry, such as draft cards, Social Security cards, library cards, credit cards, and driving licenses. They carry no identification whatsoever, and if they're stopped by the police for any reason, they give false names and no addresses. They're just "on the road," they say.

What if the police ask them for their draft cards? As one draft evader who went underground said, "We tell them we've lost our cards. If they ask where we registered, we give a false town and state, and a false local board." They carry the game as far as they can, and just hope that the FBI doesn't catch up with them.

They have friends, and their friends have friends— and through this underground network they can usually get low-paying jobs where they won't need Social Security cards, because they're paid off the books. They live in crash pads or communes, and become part of a subculture in which they can't do such ordinary things as go to school for a degree, cash a check, get a driving license, or get married.

Most of the draft evaders who choose this route are far more disillusioned with American life and values than the resisters who choose jail. After all, jail is part of "the system," and the resisters who go there believe their actions are helping to change the country. Those who go underground seem to have little hope that the country can be changed, so in effect they are abandoning it and creating a system of their own.

One young man who made the decision to go underground explained: "The thing is, of course, that resistance to the draft and the war in Vietnam are only the beginning, not an end in themselves. Because they're symptomatic of what's wrong with the system, and the system will always continue to produce things like the war and the draft. We're not just fighting those symptoms . . . we're fighting the whole mentality behind

those things, the whole value system which doesn't acknowledge the worth of human beings first . . .

"From the whole scene in the last two or three years,
the draft, the war, everything that's happened to me and
everything I've come to realize, it's pretty clear to me
that there's no place for me—no place as a human
functioning as a human and an individual—in this system, this society.

"And frankly, I don't want a place in it any more. I've
already said my good-bys."

A country is in bad enough shape when large segments
of the civilian population don't support its war effort. But
when the soldiers also start balking, the effort seems
doomed.

By the late 1960s, stories began to trickle into the
newspapers about various soldiers who were making public antiwar stands. One of them, a young doctor named
Howard Levy, was serving in the Army as a captain. He
bluntly refused orders to train Special Forces personnel
in certain medical techniques. In another case, Captain
Dale Noyd, a veteran Air Force pilot who had been carrying out combat missions for twelve years, refused orders
to train pilots for combat duty in Vietnam. He also asked
the Air Force to discharge him as a conscientious objector because he felt the war was morally wrong. Instead
of a discharge, he got a court-martial and a year in prison.

Elsewhere, two dozen soldiers tried to hold a prayer
meeting against the war in an army chapel, and several
were arrested.

Perhaps the closest thing to an organized antiwar
demonstration by soldiers was the event that took place
in 1969 at Fort Jackson, South Carolina.

Fort Jackson was no better and no worse than most

army bases. It housed a lot of new recruits who had just finished basic training and would soon be on their way to Vietnam. While they had no great enthusiasm for the war, most of them were not really opposed to it either. Mainly, they tried not to think about it.

In January 1969, Private Joe Miles was sent to Fort Jackson to attend supply school. In civilian life he had been an activist in the antiwar movement, a leader of a black students movement in Washington, D.C., and a member of the Young Socialist Alliance. He was absolutely against the war, but when he got drafted, he went.

One day, Joe asked some of his buddies in the barracks if they wanted to hear tape recordings by Malcolm X, the slain Black Muslim leader in New York. That evening, about fifteen GIs came, all of them black and Puerto Rican. They just sat around, listened to the tapes, and talked. The next night, about thirty-five soldiers showed up, again just to listen and talk.

The tapes made them think about what was happening to them—the black and the poor who were being asked to risk their lives for something they didn't really believe in—and after several more meetings they decided to form an organization. They called it GIs United Against the War in Vietnam.

White soldiers were invited to join, providing they supported the idea of black power and wanted to help end racism. The decision to admit whites had not been reached easily. The tone of the first few gatherings had been very antiwhite, but as the GIs batted around ideas and goals, they began to feel that white soldiers who were being forced to fight in Vietnam were also victims of the system.

About eighty soldiers turned out for the first interracial

meeting of GIs United, which was held right outside the barracks. The men decided to pass around a petition among all the soldiers at the base asking permission from the army brass "to hold an open meeting on post on 26 February 1969, at which all those concerned can freely discuss the legal and moral questions related to the war in Vietnam and to the civil rights of American citizens both within and outside the armed forces. It is our intention to hold a peaceful, legal meeting open to any enlisted man or officer at Fort Jackson."

In the first two days, they got about two hundred signatures on the petition, but after that, things tightened up. The commanding officers at the base found out what was going on, and turned on the pressure. Members of GIs United were harassed with such things as extra KP duty, special inspections, and restrictions.

On February 14, Joe Miles was given three hours' notice to leave Fort Jackson and report to Fort Bragg, North Carolina. He had been the driving force behind GIs United, and without him the group began to flounder. However, the men soon pulled themselves together and went ahead with the petition.

On March 3, two of the group went to post headquarters to formally present the petition to the commanding general, James F. Hollingsworth.

He wouldn't accept it. His aides read a statement refusing to acknowledge the petition, and ordered the two soldiers back to their barracks.

But this was just the beginning, for the whole country was now finding out about these events. Private José Rudder, one of the leaders of the group, described what else was happening:

"What really set the brass off was that the Huntley-

Brinkley TV News show sent a whole crew, complete with cameras, lights, and reporters, the whole bit, to Fort Jackson, South Carolina, to interview GIs United Against the War in Vietnam. And this was on national television. It was the first time that the whole country learned about GIs United, and the whole world, for that matter. Guys here on base got mail from their parents asking what was going on. It really got around, and that must have worried the brass.

"It wasn't but about four or five days later that we had our March 20 meeting where they swooped down on us."

The meeting on March 20 apparently started spontaneously. It was a beautiful evening, and several men were sitting around on the grass outside the barracks, while others were leaning out the windows. Private Rudder recalled: "I was in good spirits, and I said, 'This is a good time to rap to people.' So we started rapping. At first it was just a game, nobody thought it would develop into anything serious. We just started rapping about the war, about the Army, in a funny kind of way, cracking a few little jokes. But the guys were listening, and I began to get serious and [Private Andrew] Pulley got serious. And before we knew it, we had a full-scale GIs United meeting going on, except that this time there were maybe two hundred guys standing around, looking out the windows, coming in from the surrounding area."

At one point during the meeting, speakers were talking about the $10,000 life insurance that's given to a relative when a GI is killed. Private Rudder yelled, "Do you think $10,000 is what you're worth?" And the crowd shouted back, "No!" The meeting went on this way for a while, and then gradually broke up as the men drifted back to the barracks.

The next day, four of the spokesmen at the meeting were put in the stockade. Five other leaders of GIs United were subsequently placed under barracks arrest, and all nine faced the prospect of a court-martial and ten years at hard labor if convicted.

The charges against them were: demonstrating in uniform, demonstrating without approval of the post commander, disrespect to an officer, and breach of the peace.

Within a few days, the Army dropped all charges against one of the nine, John Huffman, who had been an outspoken leader at the March 20 meeting and a member of GIs United. It seemed that all along he had been an undercover agent, informing the Army of what the antiwar group was up to. Army officials freely admitted that he had been working for them.

The case of the Fort Jackson Nine became the case of the Fort Jackson Eight, and they were defended by a team of lawyers from the GI Civil Liberties Defense Committee, a nonprofit group.

The lawyers argued that the GIs had been acting within their constitutional rights at the meeting, because soldiers had as much right to peacefully express their views as any other Americans. If senators, congressmen, retired generals, and admirals could say that the war was wrong, why couldn't the GIs who had to fight in it?

Apparently, the Army didn't feel it had a very good case against the Fort Jackson Eight, because eventually the charges against them were dropped, and there was no court-martial. However, six were given "undesirable" discharges from the Army.

As for Private Joe Miles—who had started it all—he remained as active as ever. After being deported to Fort Bragg, he organized another branch of GIs United, which also started to circulate antiwar petitions. When the Army had all it could take of Private Miles, it sent him as far away as possible—to an army station north of the Arctic Circle.

However, putting him in cold storage couldn't stop the antiwar rumblings that were gaining momentum among American GIs. There are now other groups, other movements within the military that are loudly voicing feelings against the war.

Most alarming of all were eyewitness reports from Vietnam which said that a great many American combat soldiers were fed up with the war. In their despair and frustration, they were getting strung out on heroin and other hard drugs, which were very cheap in Vietnam. By the time the soldiers were shipped home, they were addicts—their whole future jeopardized by a demoralizing war.

Veterans, usually the most patriotic of groups, have also shown deep disillusionment with the fighting. In contrast to the proud veterans of previous wars, who joined such patriotic groups as the American Legion and the Veterans of Foreign Wars, today's ex-soldiers are rushing to join a unique antiwar group—the Vietnam Veterans Against the War. If even the soldiers and the veterans don't support this war, who does?

Despite the loud clamor and mass antiwar sentiment, the movement to end the fighting in Vietnam must still be rated a failure—just like all the other antiwar campaigns in American history. It is now four years since the American people practically forced President Johnson not to run for a second term, because they were so angered by his war policies; yet the war is still going on. The

American people's opposition may have forced the political leaders to change their rhetoric, but it has not ended the war. It is not even bringing it to a speedier conclusion. The war has been going strong since 1965—seven years! This makes it the longest war in American history, and the end is not yet in sight.

The antiwar movement reached its peak in the late 1960s, and has been losing momentum ever since. President Nixon's policy of gradual—*very* gradual—withdrawal seems to have destroyed the movement's sense of urgency. People who were throwing all their energies into antiwar work have been drifting off into other causes, such as ecology.

Yet for the American soldiers who are still fighting in Vietnam, the situation must be more painful than ever. They don't even know why they're there; all they know is that their lives are worth less than America's prestige, which requires some sort of "honorable" peace no matter how many years and how many lives it takes.

Suggested Reading

Brock, Peter, *Pacifism in the United States*. Princeton: Princeton University Press, 1968; and *20th Century Pacifism*, New York: Van Nostrand Reinhold, 1970.

Curti, Merle Eugene, *The American Peace Crusade, 1815–1860*. New York: Octagon Books, 1965; and *Bryan and World Peace*, New York: Octagon Books, 1969.

Gaylin, Dr. Willard, *In the Service of Their Country*. New York: Viking Press, 1970.

Halstead, Fred, *GI's Speak Out Against the War*. New York: Pathfinder Press, 1970.

Hentoff, Nat, *Peace Agitator, the Story of A. J. Muste*. New York: Macmillan Company, 1963.

Miller, William Robert, *Martin Luther King, Jr.* New York: Weybright and Talley, 1968.

Murdock, E., *Patriotism Limited, 1862–1865*. Ohio: Kent State University Press, 1967.

Peterson, H. C., and Fite, Gilbert C., *Opponents of War, 1917–1918*. Madison, Wisconsin: University of Wisconsin Press, 1957.

Thomas, John L., *The Liberator: William Lloyd Garrison*. Boston: Little, Brown and Company, 1963.

Villard, Oswald Garrison, *Fighting Years.* New York: Harcourt, Brace and Co., 1939.

Wittner, Lawrence S., *Rebels Against the War: the American Peace Movement, 1941–1960.* New York: Columbia University Press, 1969.

INDEX